DEFED &

WRITERS' STUDIO
Art-Based Narrative Writing Activity Book

Inspired by the art work of Justin Bua
Andre Benito Mountain & Justin Bua

FOR THE STUDENTS,

FOR THE TEACHERS,

FOR THE SCHOOL LEADERS,

FOR THE ARTISTS,

FOR THE LISTENERS,

FOR THE WRITERS,

FOR THE PROFESSORS,

FOR THE ACTIVISTS,

FOR THE CULTURE...

DEF-ED & BUA

DEF-ED & BUX

COPYRIGHT © 2024 DEF-EDUCATION LLC

All rights reserved.

Writers' Studio: Art-Based Narrative Writing Workbook

ISBN: 9798322085607

Writers' Studio

Art-Based Narrative Writing Activity Book

Andre Benito Mountain & Justin Bua

Name:

Grade Level:

4 5 6 7 8 9

Introduction to Writers' Studio:

Welcome to "Writers' Studio," a unique workbook on narrative writing that draws inspiration from the vibrant and dynamic artwork of Justin Bua. In the realm of creative expression, where visual art meets the written word, this workbook aims to unleash the power of storytelling influenced by the rich tapestry of hip-hop culture.

In recent years, there has been a growing recognition of the importance of arts-based education in fostering creativity, critical thinking, and cultural appreciation. Justin Bua's distinctive artwork, deeply rooted in the aesthetics of urban life and hip-hop culture, serves as an evocative muse for our exploration into narrative writing. Bua's mastery in capturing the essence of the streets, the rhythm of the city, and the soul of hip-hop provides a visually compelling backdrop for our journey.

Hip-hop culture, with its origins in marginalized urban communities, has evolved into a global phenomenon influencing art, music, fashion, and language. Through the lens of Justin Bua's artwork, we delve into the essence of hip-hop, exploring its impact on society, identity, and self-expression. As we navigate the vibrant streetscapes and characters within Bua's creations, we invite you to reflect on the narratives that emerge from these urban landscapes.

This workbook also pays homage to the work of Andre Benito Mountain, an educator and advocate for hip hop pedagogy. Mountain's efforts to bridge the gap between traditional school practices and the principles of hip-hop culture serve as a testament to the transformative potential of arts-based education. His work encourages us to embrace diverse forms of expression within the educational landscape and empowers students to find their voices through unconventional mediums.

As we embark on this writing journey inspired by Justin Bua's art, let us recognize the power of storytelling to change society. Narratives have the capacity to challenge norms, amplify unheard voices, and spark conversations that lead to positive transformation. Through the intersection of visual art, hip-hop culture, and narrative writing, "Urban Narratives" invites you to contribute your voice to the ongoing narrative of our urban landscapes and the diverse stories they hold. Together, let's explore the boundless possibilities of creative expression and harness the power of writing to cultivate understanding, empathy, and change in our communities.

ABOUT JUSTIN BUA

Award-winning artist, author, speaker, and entrepreneur Justin Bua is an icon in the world of art. Groundbreaking in his field, BUA is internationally known for his best-selling collection of fine art posters—The DJ being one of the most popular prints of all time.

Born in 1968 in NYC's untamed Upper West Side and raised between Manhattan and East Flatbush, Brooklyn, BUA was fascinated by the raw, visceral street life of the city. He attended the Fiorello H. LaGuardia High School of Music and Performing Arts and complemented his education on the streets by writing graffiti and performing worldwide with breakdancing crews. BUA went on to the Art Center College of Design in Pasadena, California where he earned a B.F.A. and taught figure drawing at the University of Southern California for ten years.

BUA exhibits throughout the United States and internationally—including recent shows at the Los Angeles County Museum of Art and Pop International Gallery, New York. His energetic and vocal worldwide fan base ranges from former presidents, actors, musicians, professional athletes and dancers, to street kids and art connoisseurs.

One of Bua's most celebrated series is the "The DJ" collection, where he pays homage to the influential figures of hip-hop by portraying them as modern-day warriors, guardians of a cultural legacy. Through his brushstrokes, he captures the essence of the DJ's role as a storyteller and the heartbeat of the streets. Beyond his visual art, Bua has contributed to the cultural landscape through various projects, including teaching, writing, and public speaking. His book, "The Beat of Urban Art," not only showcases his artwork but also provides insights into the stories and inspirations behind each piece, offering a deeper understanding of his creative process.

Justin Bua's impact extends far beyond the confines of the art world. His ability to seamlessly fuse urban culture with classical art has made him a trailblazer, challenging conventional notions of what art can be. Through his evocative creations, Bua invites audiences to see the beauty, struggle, and resilience found within the diverse tapestry of city life. As an artist, educator, and cultural influencer, Justin Bua has become a powerful voice, shaping the narrative of contemporary urban art and leaving an enduring legacy for generations to come.

ABOUT ANDRE BENITO MOUNTAIN

As a trailblazer in the field of education and an advocate for hip-hop pedagogy, Andre Benito Mountain stands at the forefront of a movement that seeks to bridge the gap between traditional schooling practices and the vibrant, expressive world of hip-hop culture. His work is not only transformative but also revolutionary, aiming to create educational spaces that resonate with the diverse experiences of students.

Andre Benito Mountain's journey began with a profound realization: the cultural landscape within which many students navigate their lives is not always reflected in the curriculum of traditional educational institutions. As an educator and artist, Mountain sought to rectify this gap, drawing inspiration from the dynamic and influential elements of hip-hop culture to inform his pedagogical approach.

Hip-hop, with its roots deeply embedded in urban communities, provides a powerful lens through which to explore and understand the world. Mountain recognized the potential for this cultural phenomenon to serve as a conduit for education, a tool that could engage students on a level that traditional methods often struggled to achieve. Mountain's work extends beyond the classroom, as he actively advocates for the integration of hip-hop into educational curricula. He emphasizes the importance of recognizing the cultural capital that students bring with them and incorporating it into the learning process. This approach not only validates students' experiences but also fosters a sense of empowerment and belonging within the educational environment.

Mountain's impact extends beyond the classroom walls, influencing educators, policymakers, and artists alike. He serves as a beacon for those who believe in the transformative power of education when it embraces the cultural richness of its students. In a world where diversity and inclusivity are increasingly recognized as essential components of effective education, Andre Benito Mountain's work stands as a testament to the potential for positive change. Through his dedication to hip-hop pedagogy, Mountain is not only shaping the future of education but also inspiring a generation of students to embrace their unique voices and cultural identities within the learning process.

COMPONENTS

- Justin Bua Prints w/Prompt
- Writers' Studio 4-Star Rubric
- Writers' Studio Storyboard
- Narrative Writers' Checklist
- Writing Sheets
- Writers' Studio Reading Passage
- Key Vocabulary
- Details Graphic Organizer

WRITERS' STUDIO
TABLE OF CONTENTS

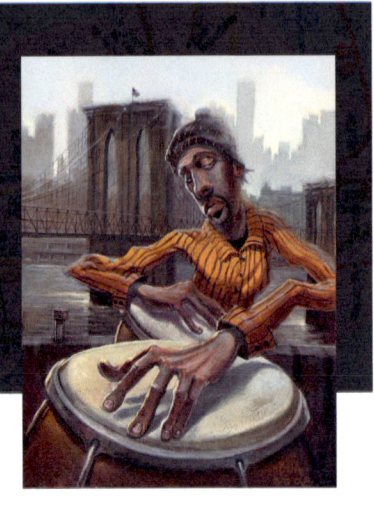

1 **WEEK 1: TIERNEY'S TESTS   1**
- Narrative Prompt
- Rubric
- Writing Sheet
- Storyboard
- Passage: The Art of Science
- Constructed Response Questions
- Key Vocabulary
- Graphic Organizer
- Weekly Reflections

2 **WEEK 2: URBAN HARMONY   15**
- Narrative Prompt
- Rubric
- Writing Sheet
- Storyboard
- Passage: Urban Harmony
- Constructed Response Questions
- Key Vocabulary
- Graphic Organizer
- Weekly Reflections

3 **WEEK 3: OLIVER   29**
- Narrative Prompt
- Rubric
- Writing Sheet
- Storyboard
- Passage: Oliver
- Constructed Response Questions
- Key Vocab
- Graphic Organizer
- Weekly Reflections

4 **WEEK 4: ENCHANTED DRUMS   43**
- Narrative Prompt
- Rubric
- Writing Sheet
- Storyboard
- Passage: Enchanted Drums
- Constructed Response Questions
- Key Vocabulary
- Graphic Organizer
- Weekly Reflections

WRITERS' STUDIO
TABLE OF CONTENTS

5 — WEEK 5: ELLA'S GIFT   54
- Narrative Prompt..
- Rubric
- Writing Sheet
- Storyboard
- Passage: Ella's Gift
- Constructed Response Questions
- Key Vocabulary
- Graphic Organizer
- Weekly Reflections

6 — WEEK 6: JOE COLLIER & THE GODFATHER   67
- Narrative Prompt..
- Rubric
- Writing Sheet
- Storyboard
- Passage: Joe Collier & the Godfather
- Constructed Response Questions
- Key Vocabulary
- Graphic Organizer
- Weekly Reflections

7 — WEEK 7: CARLOS & THE COLLECTION   82
- Narrative Prompt..
- Rubric
- Writing Sheet
- Storyboard
- Passage: Carlos & the Collection
- Constructed Response Questions
- Key Vocabulary
- Graphic Organizer
- Weekly Reflections

8 — WEEK 8: JAZZ, HIP-HOP AND THE BROWNSTONE'S TIMELESS ECHO   94
- Narrative Prompt..
- Rubric
- Writing Sheet
- Storyboard
- Passage: Jazz, Hip-Hop and the Brownstone's Timeless Echo
- Constructed Response Questions
- Key Vocabulary
- Graphic Organizer
- Weekly Reflections

WRITERS' STUDIO
TABLE OF CONTENTS

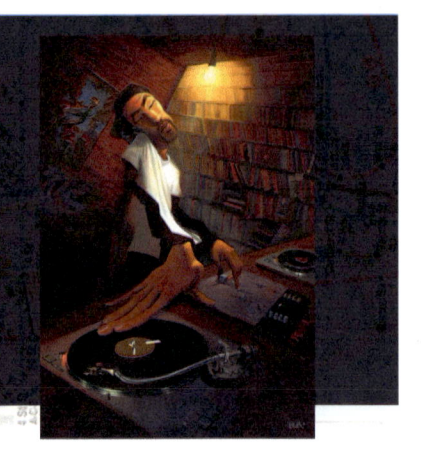

9 | WEEK 9: JEFFREY'S JOURNEY   107
- Narrative Prompt
- Rubric
- Writing Sheet
- Storyboard
- Passage: Jeffrey's Journey
- Constructed Response Questions
- Key Vocabulary
- Graphic Organizer
- Weekly Reflections

10 | WEEK 10: COASTAL DREAMS 121
- Narrative Prompt
- Rubric
- Writing Sheet
- Storyboard
- Passage: Coastal Dreams
- Constructed Response Questions
- Key Vocabulary
- Graphic Organizer
- Weekly Reflections

THE HIP HOP LITERACY LAB

DEF-EDUCATION LLC

Week 1: Tierney's Tests

NARRATIVE PROMPT:
A young scientist makes a discovery that will improve the lives of children in an amazing way. Write an original story that describes her discovery and how she plans to use it.

DEF-EDUCATION LLC

Writers' Studio 4-Star Rubric

04 ★★★★

- The student's response uses the image as a stimulus to completely create a genuine or imagined experience through a well-developed narrative.
- Uses a variety of words and phrases to signal the sequence of events;
- Consistently conveys experiences or events precisely through the use of concrete words, phrases, and sensory language;
- Provides a conclusion that follows from the narrated experiences or events;
- Integrates ideas and details from source material in an effective manner;

03 ★★★

- The student's response uses the text as a trigger to create a whole narrative that describes a real or imagined experience.
- Establishes a scene and introduces one or more characters;
- lays out the events in a clear, logical sequence; employs narrative devices, like dialogue and description, to develop experiences and events or illustrate how characters react to them;
- uses words and/or phrases to denote sequence;
- conveys experiences and events with words, phrases, and details; offers a suitable resolution

02 ★★

- The student's answer, which used the image as a stimulus, is an incomplete or simplistic story.
- It attempts to use a narrative technique, such as dialogue or description, to develop experiences and events or show the responses of characters to situations.
- It introduces a vague situation and at least one character.
- It organizes events in a sequence but with some gaps or ambiguity.
- It uses sporadic signal words to indicate sequence. It uses some words or phrases inconsistently to convey experiences and events.
- Finally, it offers a weak or unclear resolution.

01 ★

- The student's response shows that they attempted to use the material as a stimulus to compose a narrative.
- The response summarises the plot; it introduces a character or scenario in a weak or basic way; it may be too short to show the whole chain of events.
- It employs language that is inappropriate, excessively simple, or unclear; it provides few, if any, words that convey experiences or events;
- it provides little to no conclusion;
- it makes little to no attempt to use dialogue or description to develop experiences and events or show the responses of characters to situations; and it may use few, if any, ideas or details from the source material.

DEF-EDUCATION LLC

Narrative Writer's Checklist

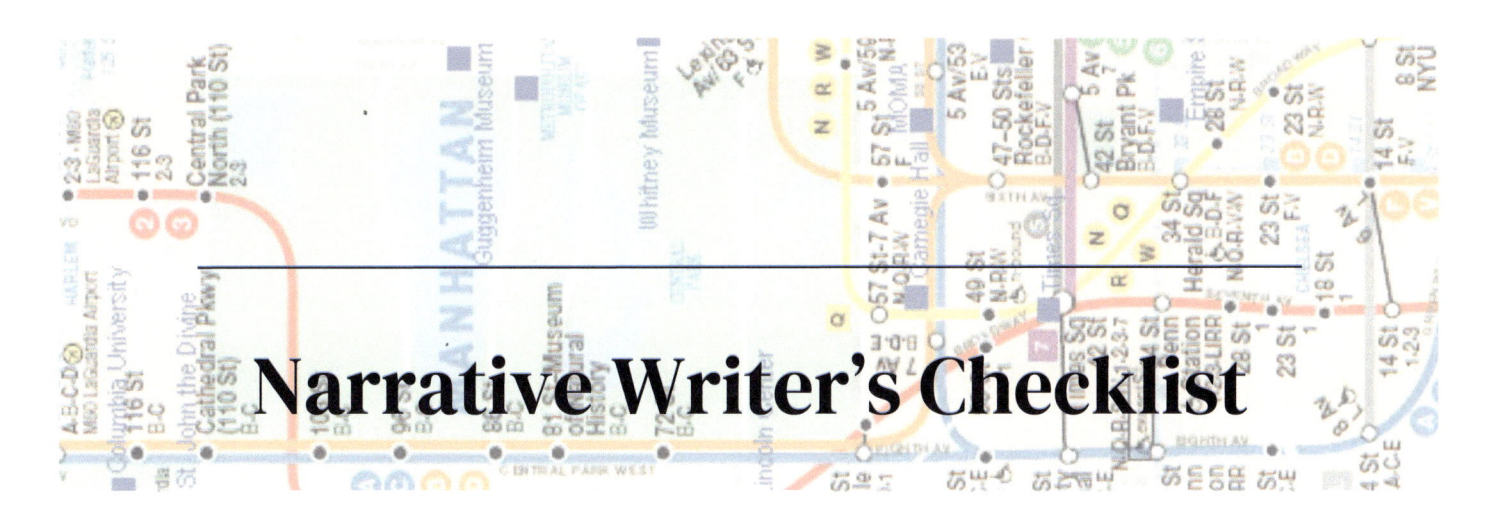

01	Develop a real or imagined experience in the form of a narrative.	☐
02	Include a situation and introduce a narrator and/or characters.	☐
03	Use words and phrases to show the sequence of events.	☐

04	Use dialogue and/or descriptions of actions, thoughts, and emotions to:
	   o develop events.
	   o show how characters respond to situations.
		☐

05	Check your work for correct usage, grammar, spelling, capitalization, and punctuation.	☐
06	Organize events in chronological order.	☐
07	Include a conclusion.	☐

NARRATIVE PROMPT:

A young scientist makes a discovery that will improve the lives of children in an amazing way. Write an original story that describes her discovery and how she plans to use it.

Writers' Studio Storyboard

Develop a featured image for your narrative.

Title:

Medium(s) Used:

Writers' Studio Storyboard

Develop a storyboard for your narrative.

TIERNEY'S TESTS

Lexile Range: 1210L-1400L

Directions: Read the passage and write a summary of the main events, including details.

In the bustling metropolis of Atlanta, amidst the rhythm of the city and the vibrant beats of hip hop, lived a young and brilliant scientist named Tierney. She wasn't your typical scientist—Tierney had a passion that set her apart. Beyond her love for equations and experiments, she was a talented artist, drawing inspiration from the dynamic and diverse culture that surrounded her.

Tierney's days were spent in a laboratory, where she delved into the mysteries of science. By night, she immersed herself in the beats and rhymes of hip hop, a culture that resonated with her soul. The graffiti-covered walls of Atlanta spoke to her in vibrant colors, telling stories of resilience and creativity. This fusion of science and art, of logic and expression, made Tierney a unique force in the world of discovery. One day, while working tirelessly in her lab, Tierney stumbled upon a breakthrough that would change the lives of children forever. In her pursuit of scientific excellence, she uncovered a groundbreaking solution to a common challenge faced by young minds struggling to learn and express themselves.

Tierney had discovered a way to combine the principles of hip hop with educational science. She realized that the rhythmic patterns and storytelling inherent in hip hop could serve as a powerful tool for teaching and engaging young minds. Inspired by the culture she loved, Tierney developed an innovative program that used hip hop to enhance literacy and numeracy skills in children.

Her program wasn't just about rhymes and rhythms; it was a holistic approach that embraced the entire hip hop culture. From beatboxing to graffiti-style visual aids, Tierney's lessons were infused with the creativity and vibrancy that made hip hop a global phenomenon. As a talented artist herself, Tierney understood the importance of providing an avenue for self-expression, allowing each child to discover their unique voice.

TIERNEY'S TESTS (CONTINUED)

Lexile Range: 1210L-1400L

Directions: Read the passage and write a summary of the main events, including details.

Word of Tierney's groundbreaking discovery spread throughout Atlanta, and soon her program gained traction in schools and communities. Children who once struggled to connect with traditional learning methods found joy and inspiration in Tierney's innovative approach. The rhythm of hip hop became the heartbeat of their education, transforming their understanding of language, mathematics, and creativity.
Tierney's dual identity as a scientist and artist proved to be the perfect synergy for this groundbreaking initiative. Her love for hip hop had not only shaped her as an individual but had also become a catalyst for positive change in the lives of countless children.

In the heart of Atlanta, where the beats of hip hop echoed through the streets, Tierney's discovery became a testament to the power of embracing diversity and weaving it into the fabric of education. She had created a harmonious blend of science, art, and culture that echoed the spirit of hip hop—resilient, creative, and capable of changing the world, one child at a time.

COMPREHENSION QUESTIONS

DOK 3 (Strategic Thinking) Questions:

1. How does Tierney's dual passion for science and hip-hop contribute to her unique perspective on education?

2. Analyze the role of Atlanta's vibrant culture in shaping Tierney's approach to her scientific discoveries and artistic endeavors.

3. Evaluate the implications of Tierney's breakthrough discovery on traditional methods of teaching. How does it challenge and transform current educational practices?

4. Compare and contrast Tierney's innovative program with traditional teaching methods. In what ways does it offer a strategic and transformative alternative?

5. Examine the elements of Tierney's educational program inspired by hip-hop. How do these elements engage students in learning?

COMPREHENSION QUESTIONS

DOK 4 (Extended Thinking) Questions:

1. Assess the potential long-term societal impact of Tierney's program on the children who participate. How might it influence their academic and personal trajectories?

2. Synthesize the various components of Tierney's hip-hop-inspired education program and propose additional innovative elements that could further enhance its effectiveness.

3. Investigate potential challenges or criticisms that Tierney's program might face in a broader educational context. How could these challenges be addressed to ensure sustained success?

4. Develop a comprehensive plan for implementing Tierney's program on a larger scale, considering factors such as community involvement, teacher training, and sustainability.

5. Formulate a research question based on Tierney's story, exploring how hip-hop-infused educational methods might be adapted and applied in diverse cultural and educational settings globally.

KEY VOCABULARY

Use context clues to determine the meaning of each term below from the text.
Next, use a device or dictionary to determine the meaning of each term.

- **inherent**

- **harmonious**

- **holistic**

- **dual**

- **vibrancy**

Details GRAPHIC ORGANIZER

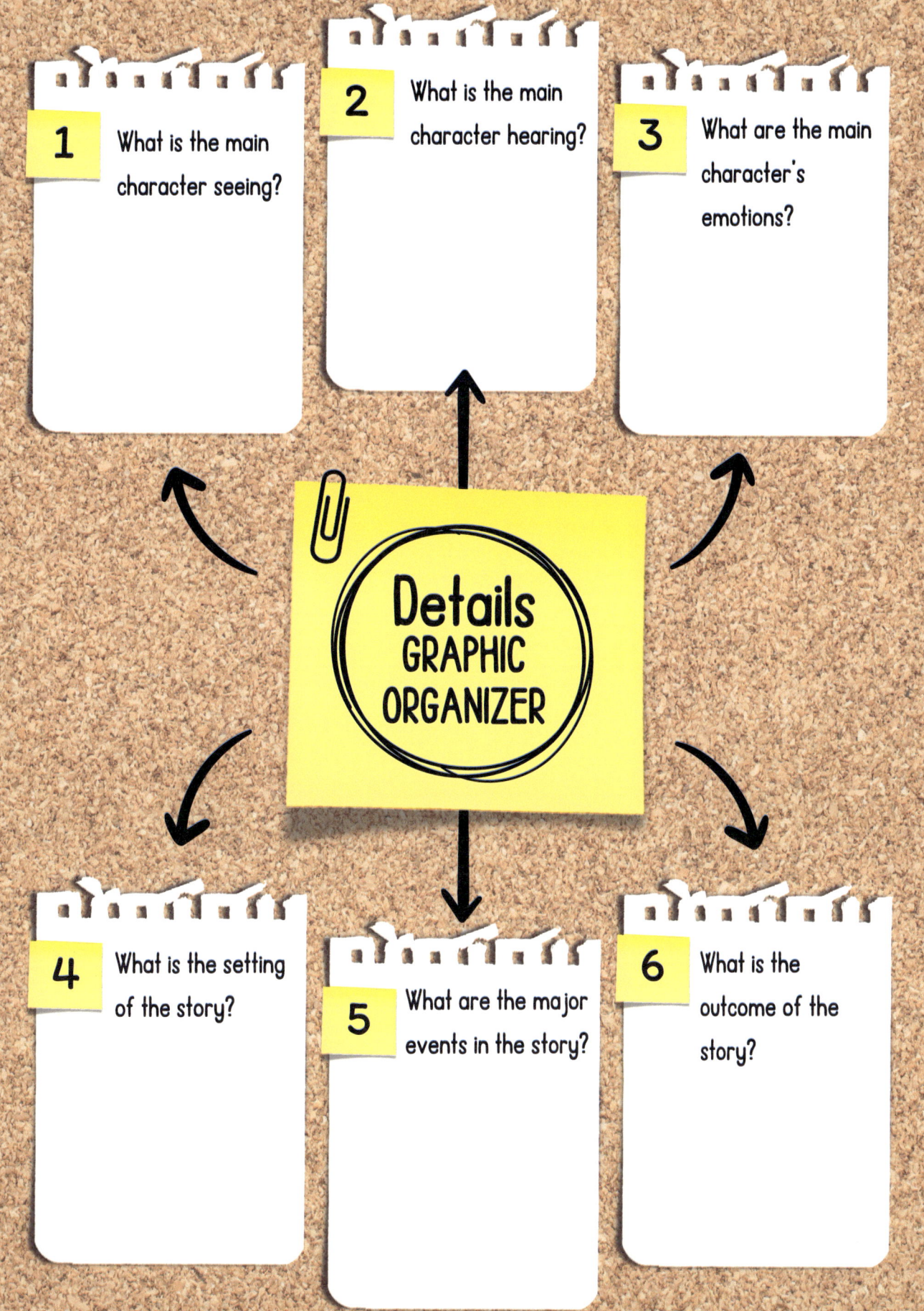

1. What is the main character seeing?

2. What is the main character hearing?

3. What are the main character's emotions?

4. What is the setting of the story?

5. What are the major events in the story?

6. What is the outcome of the story?

WRITERS' STUDIO
WEEKLY REFLECTIONS

NAME:	DATE:

ACHIEVEMENTS
What were the top three things I accomplished this week?

CHALLENGES
What did I learn from facing these challenges?

GROWTH INSIGHTS
An area I want to improve is…

KEY LEARNINGS
Goals accomplished..

TIME & BALANCE
How effectively did I manage my time?

Week 2: Urban Harmony

NARRATIVE PROMPT:
Four brothers possess an incredible talent that inspires many. Write a narrative about the talent they possess and what they do to share it with the world.

Writers' Studio 4-Star Rubric

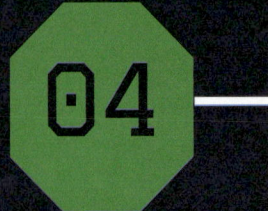

04 ★★★★

- The student's response uses the image as a stimulus to completely create a genuine or imagined experience through a well-developed narrative.
- Uses a variety of words and phrases to signal the sequence of events;
- Consistently conveys experiences or events precisely through the use of concrete words, phrases, and sensory language;
- Provides a conclusion that follows from the narrated experiences or events;
- Integrates ideas and details from source material in an effective manner;

03 ★★★

- The student's response uses the text as a trigger to create a whole narrative that describes a real or imagined experience.
- Establishes a scene and introduces one or more characters;
- lays out the events in a clear, logical sequence; employs narrative devices, like dialogue and description, to develop experiences and events or illustrate how characters react to them;
- uses words and/or phrases to denote sequence;
- conveys experiences and events with words, phrases, and details; offers a suitable resolution

02 ★★

- The student's answer, which used the image as a stimulus, is an incomplete or simplistic story.
- It attempts to use a narrative technique, such as dialogue or description, to develop experiences and events or show the responses of characters to situations.
- It introduces a vague situation and at least one character.
- It organizes events in a sequence but with some gaps or ambiguity.
- It uses sporadic signal words to indicate sequence. It uses some words or phrases inconsistently to convey experiences and events.
- Finally, it offers a weak or unclear resolution.

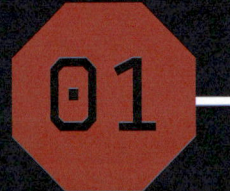

01 ★

- The student's response shows that they attempted to use the material as a stimulus to compose a narrative.
- The response summarises the plot; it introduces a character or scenario in a weak or basic way; it may be too short to show the whole chain of events.
- It employs language that is inappropriate, excessively simple, or unclear; it provides few, if any, words that convey experiences or events;
- it provides little to no conclusion;
- it makes little to no attempt to use dialogue or description to develop experiences and events or show the responses of characters to situations; and it may use few, if any, ideas or details from the source material.

Narrative Writer's Checklist

01	Develop a real or imagined experience.	☐
02	Include a situation and introduce a narrator and/or characters.	☐
03	Use words and phrases to show the sequence of events.	☐
04	Use dialogue and/or descriptions of actions, thoughts, and feelings to: 　o develop events. 　o show how characters respond to situations.	☐
05	Check your work for correct usage, grammar, spelling, capitalization, and punctuation.	☐
06	Organize events in order.	☐
07	Include a conclusion.	☐

NARRATIVE PROMPT:
Four brothers possess an incredible talent that inspires many. Write a narrative about the talent they possess and what they do to share it with the world.

Writers' Studio Storyboard

Develop a featured image for your narrative.

Title:
Medium(s) Used:

Writers' Studio Storyboard

Develop a storyboard for your narrative.

URBAN HARMONY

Lexile Range: 1210L-1400L

Directions: Read the passage and write a summary of the main events, including details.

Hip Hop is a music and culture that gives voice to many youth. Atlanta has established itself as a city whose unique sound adds texture to the culture of Hip Hop. In the heart of Atlanta, where the rhythm of the city pulses through the streets like a constant beat, four aspiring rappers emerged from the vibrant **tapestry** of the urban landscape. Their names were Malik, Jazz, Marcus, and Nasir – a diverse group with dreams as vast as the city skyline.

Each rapper brought a unique flavor to the group, reflecting the **eclectic** mix of cultures and influences that defined Atlanta's music scene. Malik, with his sharp lyrics and gritty storytelling, embodied the spirit of the city's streets. Jazz, with his melodic flow and empowering rhymes, brought a touch of soul to the group. Marcus, the **wordsmith**, wove intricate verses that showcased his love for the art of rap. Nasir, the firecracker, spit rapid-fire verses that captivated audiences with his energy and **charisma**.

Together, they formed a tight-knit crew, determined to not only make their mark in the competitive world of hip-hop but also to uplift their community through their music. They called themselves "Urban Harmony" – a nod to their diverse backgrounds and a commitment to finding unity in the midst of diversity.

Their journey began in the underground clubs and open mic nights scattered throughout Atlanta. Night after night, they honed their skills and fine-tuned their sound, gaining respect and admiration from fellow artists and fans alike. But for Urban Harmony, success wasn't just about fame and fortune; it was about using their platform to inspire positive change.

URBAN HARMONY

Lexile Range: 1210L-1400L

Directions: Read the passage and write a summary of the main events, including details.

One day, they decided to organize a series of free workshops for aspiring young artists in the city. They shared their experiences, offered guidance on navigating the music industry, and emphasized the importance of staying true to oneself. The workshops became a catalyst for a new wave of talent in Atlanta, fostering a sense of community among budding artists.

Urban Harmony's music echoed the struggles and triumphs of everyday life in Atlanta. Their lyrics spoke of resilience, hope, and the power of unity. Whether performing in local schools, community centers, or major venues, they used their platform to shine a light on the issues that mattered most to their community. As their popularity grew, so did their impact. Urban Harmony became advocates for education and social justice, using their influence to support local initiatives and charities. They organized charity concerts, donating proceeds to causes ranging from youth empowerment programs to community development projects.

Atlanta began to see a positive transformation, with the spirit of Urban Harmony resonating throughout the city. The four rappers became role models for aspiring artists, proving that success could be achieved not only through talent but also through authenticity, collaboration, and a genuine commitment to making a difference.

In the end, Urban Harmony's journey wasn't just a story of four rappers finding success in the music industry; it was a testament to the **transformative** power of art and the ability of passionate individuals to inspire change in the world around them.

COMPREHENSION QUESTIONS

DOK 2 (Understanding) Questions:

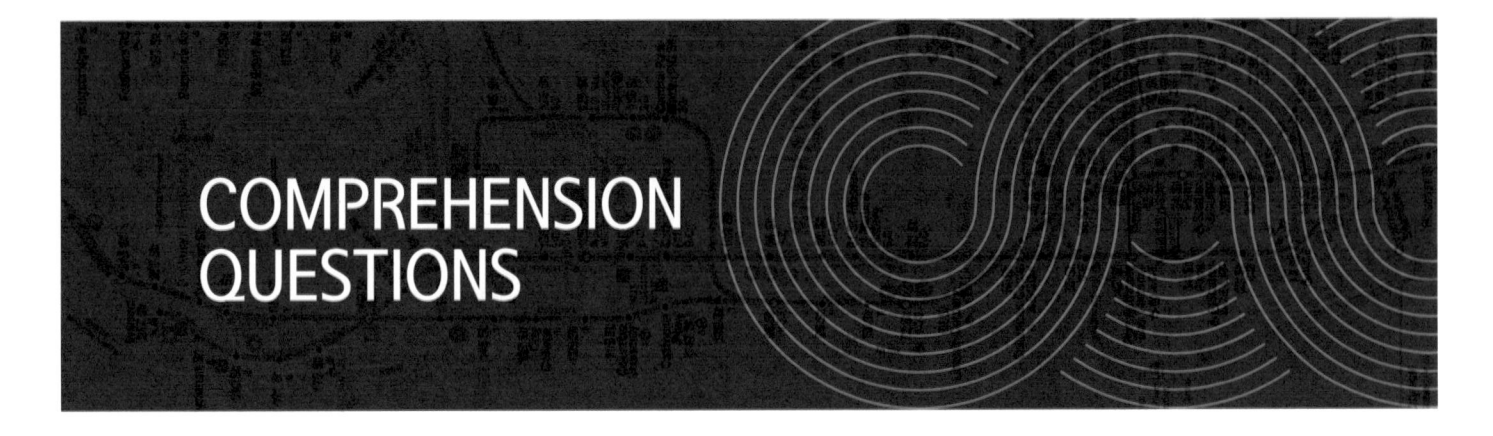

1. How does the passage describe each member of Urban Harmony and the unique contributions they bring to the group?

2. Explain the significance of the name "Urban Harmony" and how it reflects the diversity and commitment of the group.

DOK 3 (Strategic Thinking) Questions:

1. Analyze the challenges Urban Harmony faced as they pursued success in the hip-hop industry. How did their commitment to positive change distinguish them from other aspiring artists?

2. Consider the impact of Urban Harmony's free workshops on the local music community. How did these workshops contribute to fostering a sense of community and supporting emerging talent in Atlanta?

3. Evaluate the role of Urban Harmony's lyrics in reflecting the essence of life in Atlanta. How did their music serve as a vehicle for addressing important social issues, and what impact did it have on their audience?

KEY VOCABULARY

Use context clues to determine the meaning of each term below from the text.
Next, use a device or dictionary to determine the meaning of each term.

- **transformative**

- **charisma**

- **wordsmith**

- **tapestry**

- **showcased**

KEY VOCABULARY

- **genuine**

- **empowerment**

- **uplift**

- **eclectic**

- **resilience**

Details GRAPHIC ORGANIZER

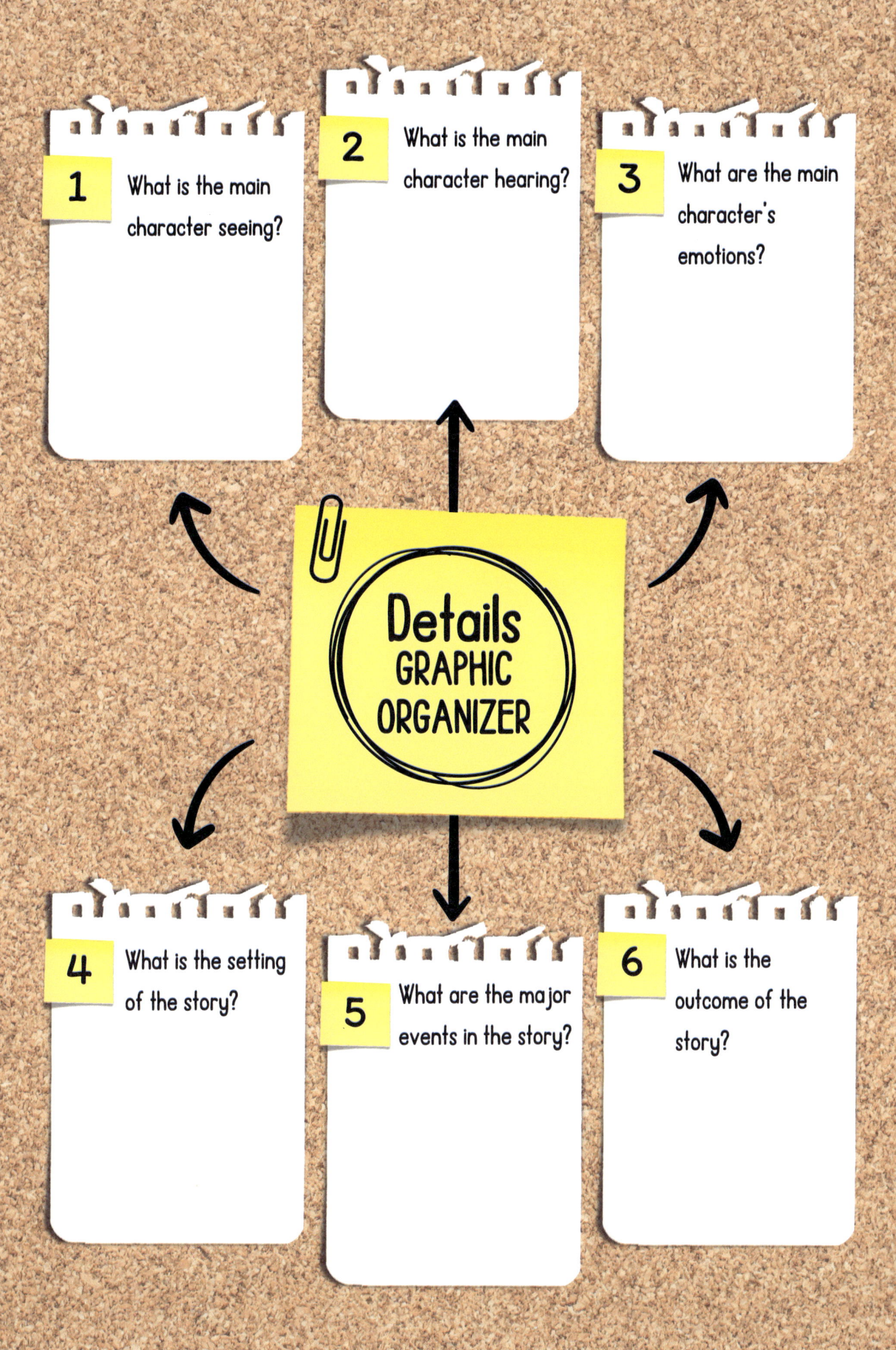

1. What is the main character seeing?

2. What is the main character hearing?

3. What are the main character's emotions?

4. What is the setting of the story?

5. What are the major events in the story?

6. What is the outcome of the story?

WRITERS' STUDIO
WEEKLY REFLECTIONS

NAME: DATE:

ACHIEVEMENTS
What were the top three things I accomplished this week?

CHALLENGES
What did I learn from facing these challenges?

GROWTH INSIGHTS
An area I want to improve is...

KEY LEARNINGS
Goals accomplished..

TIME & BALANCE
How effectively did I manage my time?

Week 3: Oliver

NARRATIVE PROMPT:
Write a narrative about a man who has discovered that he can communicate with butterflies. Write an original story about how he discovers this ability and what happens next.

Writers' Studio 4-Star Rubric

04 ★★★★

- The student's response uses the image as a stimulus to completely create a genuine or imagined experience through a well-developed narrative.
- Uses a variety of words and phrases to signal the sequence of events;
- Consistently conveys experiences or events precisely through the use of concrete words, phrases, and sensory language;
- Provides a conclusion that follows from the narrated experiences or events;
- Integrates ideas and details from source material in an effective manner;

03 ★★★

- The student's response uses the text as a trigger to create a whole narrative that describes a real or imagined experience.
- Establishes a scene and introduces one or more characters;
- lays out the events in a clear, logical sequence; employs narrative devices, like dialogue and description, to develop experiences and events or illustrate how characters react to them;
- uses words and/or phrases to denote sequence;
- conveys experiences and events with words, phrases, and details; offers a suitable resolution

02 ★★

- The student's answer, which used the image as a stimulus, is an incomplete or simplistic story.
- It attempts to use a narrative technique, such as dialogue or description, to develop experiences and events or show the responses of characters to situations.
- It introduces a vague situation and at least one character.
- It organizes events in a sequence but with some gaps or ambiguity.
- It uses sporadic signal words to indicate sequence. It uses some words or phrases inconsistently to convey experiences and events.
- Finally, it offers a weak or unclear resolution.

01 ★

- The student's response shows that they attempted to use the material as a stimulus to compose a narrative.
- The response summarises the plot; it introduces a character or scenario in a weak or basic way; it may be too short to show the whole chain of events.
- It employs language that is inappropriate, excessively simple, or unclear; it provides few, if any, words that convey experiences or events;
- it provides little to no conclusion;
- it makes little to no attempt to use dialogue or description to develop experiences and events or show the responses of characters to situations; and it may use few, if any, ideas or details from the source material.

Narrative Writer's Checklist

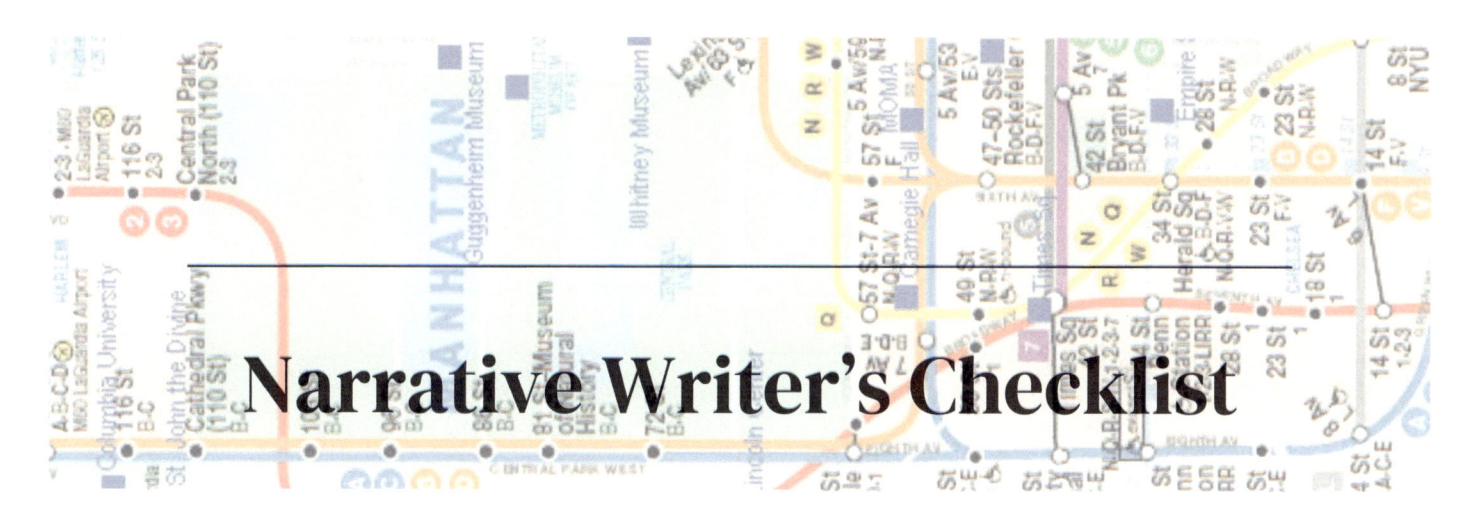

01	Develop a real or imagined experience. ☐
02	Include a situation and introduce a narrator and/or characters. ☐
03	Use words and phrases to show the sequence of events. ☐
04	Use dialogue and/or descriptions of actions, thoughts, and feelings to: 　o develop events. 　o show how characters respond to situations. ☐
05	Check your work for correct usage, grammar, spelling, capitalization, and punctuation. ☐
06	Organize events in order. ☐
07	Include a conclusion. ☐

NARRATIVE PROMPT:
Write a narrative about a man who has discovered that he can communicate with butterflies. Write an original story about how he discovers this ability and what happens next.

Writers' Studio Storyboard

Develop a featured image for your narrative.

Title:
Medium(s) Used:

Writers' Studio Storyboard

Develop a storyboard for your narrative.

OLIVER

Lexile Range: 1010L - 1200L

Directions: Read the passage and write a summary of the main events, including details.

Once upon a time, in a small village nestled between rolling hills and meandering streams, there lived a man named Oliver. Oliver was an ordinary man with an extraordinary fascination for butterflies. His love for these delicate creatures was so profound that he spent most of his days wandering through fields and forests, observing their vibrant colors and graceful dances.

One sunny afternoon, as Oliver strolled through a wildflower-filled meadow, he noticed three particularly enchanting butterflies. Their wings shimmered with a mesmerizing blend of blue, purple, and gold. Intrigued, Oliver watched as they fluttered and danced in perfect harmony. He felt an inexplicable connection to these butterflies, as if they carried a message meant just for him.

As the days passed, Oliver's bond with the butterflies deepened. He began to notice that whenever he faced challenges or uncertainties, the three butterflies would appear, swirling around him like ethereal companions. They became his source of inspiration, guiding him through the highs and lows of life.

One day, while exploring a dense forest, Oliver stumbled upon an ancient-looking tree with gnarled branches and a mysterious aura. As he approached, the three butterflies circled around the tree, their delicate wings creating a magical spectacle. Curiosity overcoming him, Oliver reached out to touch the bark, and a surge of energy coursed through his veins.

To his astonishment, the ancient tree began to shimmer, revealing a hidden doorway that led to a magical realm. The butterflies led Oliver through this enchanted passage into a land of wonder, where trees whispered ancient tales and flowers sang sweet melodies.

OLIVER

Lexile Range: 1010L - 1200L

Directions: Read the passage and write a summary of the main events, including details.

In this mystical realm, Oliver discovered that the butterflies were not ordinary creatures but magical guardians. They bestowed upon him the gift of insight and the ability to communicate with nature. Oliver became a bridge between the human world and the magical realm, ensuring balance and harmony.

As the years passed, Oliver shared his newfound knowledge with the villagers, teaching them to respect and cherish the natural world around them. The village prospered, and the once-hidden magic of the land flourished with each passing season.

One day, as Oliver stood at the edge of the meadow where his journey began, he felt a gentle breeze. The three butterflies, now radiant and more vibrant than ever, fluttered gracefully around him. With a sense of gratitude, Oliver bid them farewell, knowing that their purpose in his life had been fulfilled.

The magical realm gradually faded from view, but Oliver's connection with nature remained strong. He continued to inspire generations to come, leaving behind a legacy of love for the natural world and the belief that even the smallest creatures, like three enchanting butterflies, could lead to the most extraordinary adventures.

COMPREHENSION QUESTIONS

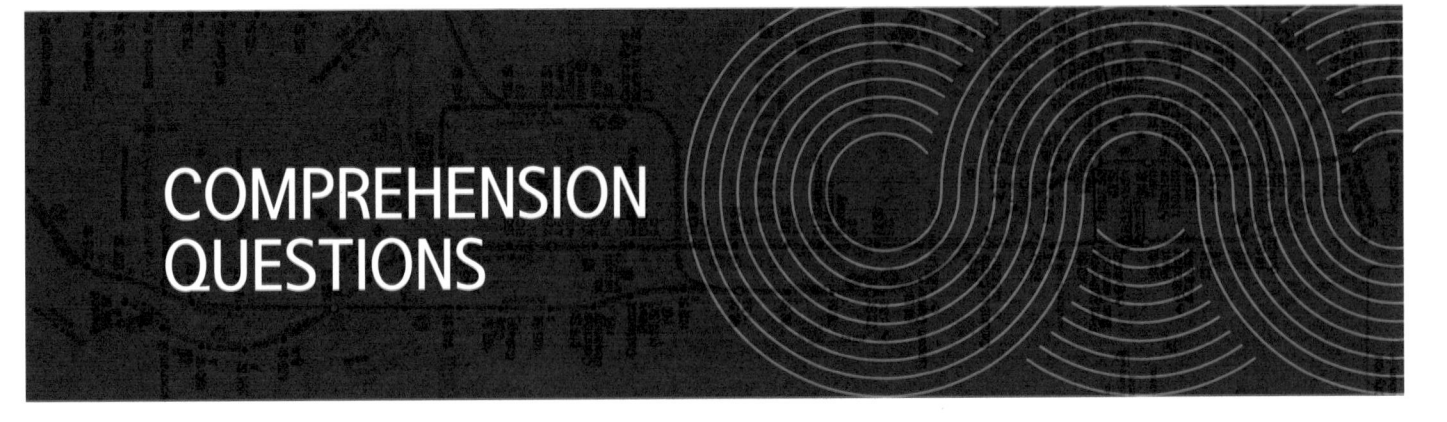

DOK 2 (Understanding) Questions:

1. Describe Oliver's initial fascination with butterflies and how it evolves throughout the passage.

2. Explain the significance of the three butterflies in Oliver's life. How do they become his companions and a source of inspiration?

DOK 3 (Strategic Thinking) Questions:

1. Analyze the role of the ancient tree in the story and its connection to Oliver's journey. How does the discovery of the magical realm impact Oliver's understanding of the natural world?

2. Consider Oliver's transformation into a bridge between the human world and the magical realm. How does this newfound ability contribute to the overall balance and harmony in the story?

3. Evaluate Oliver's impact on the village and the natural world. How does he use his knowledge to inspire the villagers, and what positive changes result from his teachings?

KEY VOCABULARY

Use context clues to determine the meaning of each term below from the text.
Next, use a device or dictionary to determine the meaning of each term.

- **insight**

- **cherish**

- **radiant**

- **spectacle**

- **ethereal**

KEY VOCABULARY

Use context clues to determine the meaning of each term below from the text.
Next, use a device or dictionary to determine the meaning of each term.

- **Vibrant**

- **Inexplicable**

- **newfound**

- **mystical**

- **gratitude**

Details GRAPHIC ORGANIZER

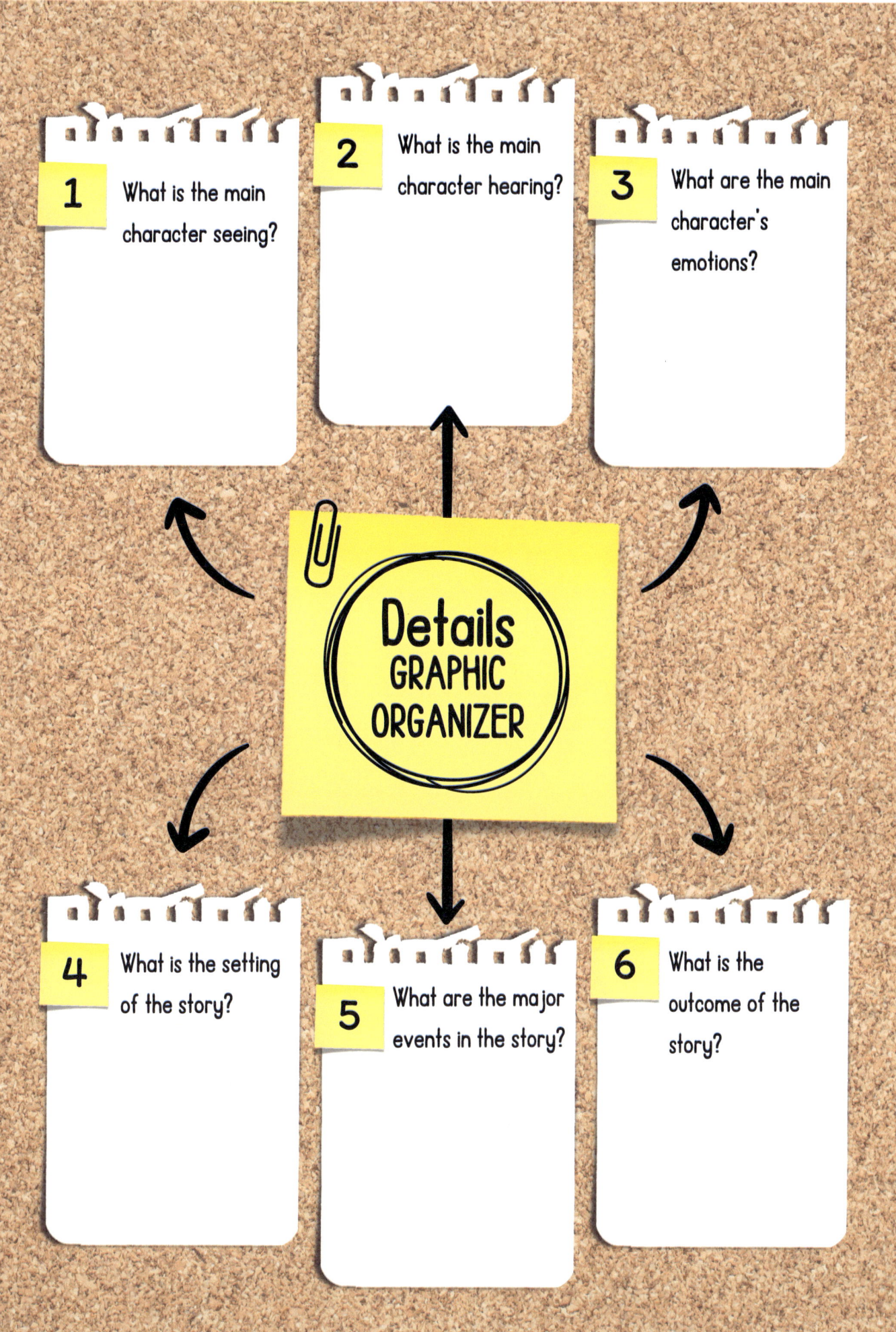

1. What is the main character seeing?

2. What is the main character hearing?

3. What are the main character's emotions?

4. What is the setting of the story?

5. What are the major events in the story?

6. What is the outcome of the story?

WRITERS' STUDIO

Weekly Reflections

NAME: DATE:

ACHIEVEMENTS
What were the top three things I accomplished this week?

CHALLENGES
What did I learn from facing these challenges?

GROWTH INSIGHTS
An area I want to improve is...

KEY LEARNINGS
Goals accomplished..

TIME & BALANCE
How effectively did I manage my time?

Week 4: Enchanted Drums

NARRATIVE PROMPT:
A drummer discovers a set of drums that take the drummer back in time when he plays them. Write a story about what happens when he starts to play the drums one Saturday morning.

Writers' Studio 4-Star Rubric

04 ★★★★

- The student's response uses the image as a stimulus to completely create a genuine or imagined experience through a well-developed narrative.
- Uses a variety of words and phrases to signal the sequence of events;
- Consistently conveys experiences or events precisely through the use of concrete words, phrases, and sensory language;
- Provides a conclusion that follows from the narrated experiences or events;
- Integrates ideas and details from source material in an effective manner;

03 ★★★

- The student's response uses the text as a trigger to create a whole narrative that describes a real or imagined experience.
- Establishes a scene and introduces one or more characters;
- lays out the events in a clear, logical sequence; employs narrative devices, like dialogue and description, to develop experiences and events or illustrate how characters react to them;
- uses words and/or phrases to denote sequence;
- conveys experiences and events with words, phrases, and details; offers a suitable resolution

02 ★★

- The student's answer, which used the image as a stimulus, is an incomplete or simplistic story.
- It attempts to use a narrative technique, such as dialogue or description, to develop experiences and events or show the responses of characters to situations.
- It introduces a vague situation and at least one character.
- It organizes events in a sequence but with some gaps or ambiguity.
- It uses sporadic signal words to indicate sequence. It uses some words or phrases inconsistently to convey experiences and events.
- Finally, it offers a weak or unclear resolution.

01 ★

- The student's response shows that they attempted to use the material as a stimulus to compose a narrative.
- The response summarises the plot; it introduces a character or scenario in a weak or basic way; it may be too short to show the whole chain of events.
- It employs language that is inappropriate, excessively simple, or unclear; it provides few, if any, words that convey experiences or events;
- it provides little to no conclusion;
- it makes little to no attempt to use dialogue or description to develop experiences and events or show the responses of characters to situations; and it may use few, if any, ideas or details from the source material.

Narrative Writer's Checklist

- Develop a real or imagined experience. ☐

- Include a situation and introduce a narrator and/or characters. ☐

- Use words and phrases to show the sequence of events. ☐

- Use dialogue and/or descriptions of actions, thoughts, and feelings to: ☐
    - o develop events.
    - o show how characters respond to situations.

- Check your work for correct usage, grammar, spelling, capitalization, and punctuation. ☐

- Organize events in order. ☐

- Include a conclusion. ☐

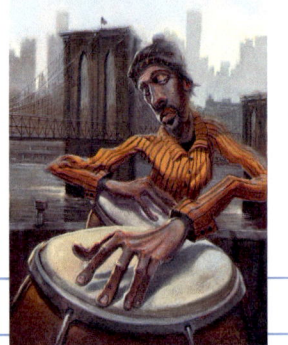

NARRATIVE PROMPT:

A drummer discovers a set of drums that take the drummer back in time when he plays them. Write a story about what happens when he starts to play the drums one Saturday morning.

Writers' Studio Storyboard

Develop a featured image for your narrative.

Title:
Medium(s) Used:

Writers' Studio Storyboard

Develop a storyboard for your narrative.

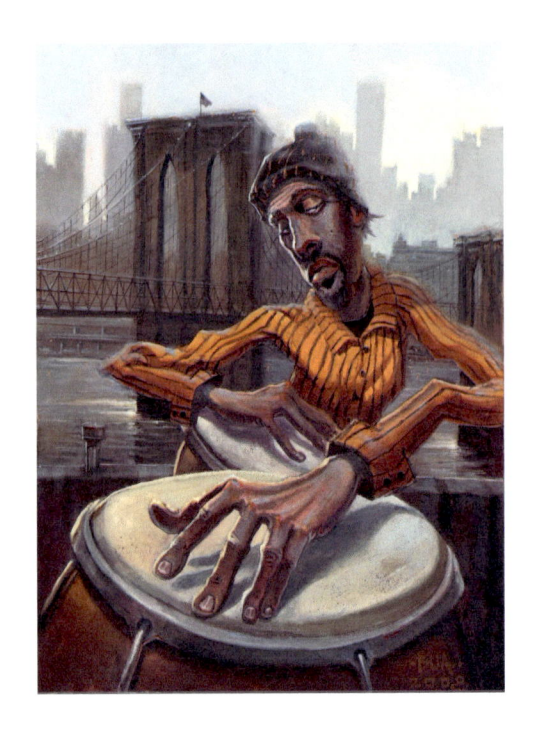

ENCHANTED DRUMS

Lexile Range: 1010L - 1200L

Directions: Read the passage and write a summary of the main events, including details.

Once upon a time in a small town, there lived a little drummer boy named Timmy. Timmy loved playing his drums more than anything else in the world. Every day, he would sit on his porch, drumming away with all his heart, filling the air with joyful beats.

One sunny day, while Timmy was exploring the attic of his house, he stumbled upon two old and dusty drums. They seemed ordinary at first, but when Timmy started playing them, something magical happened. The beats of the drums transported him through time! Excitement bubbled within Timmy as he found himself in a bustling town square, surrounded by people wearing clothes from long ago. The magical drums had taken him back in time! Timmy marveled at the sights and sounds of the past, but he knew he couldn't stay forever.

He played the drums again, and with a powerful beat, he returned to his own time. Timmy was amazed at the possibilities these magical drums held. He decided to use them to explore different times in history, learning about ancient civilizations, meeting legendary figures, and experiencing the wonders of the past.

One day, while drumming in the time of knights and dragons, Timmy met a friendly dragon who loved the sound of his drums. Together, they formed a drumming duo that echoed through the medieval lands. The people in that time loved their music and celebrated with grand feasts.

As Timmy continued his time-traveling adventures, he discovered that the magical drums not only allowed him to explore history but also to share the joy of music across different ages. In ancient Egypt, he played for pharaohs and their majestic pyramids. In the wild west, his rhythmic beats echoed through dusty towns, bringing smiles to faces.

ENCHANTED DRUMS

Lexile Range: 1010L - 1200L

Directions: Read the passage and write a summary of the main events, including details.

Timmy's magical drumming even helped resolve conflicts. In a faraway kingdom, he played a calming rhythm that united warring factions, bringing about peace and harmony. The power of music, carried by the enchanted drums, had a magical effect on people's hearts. Eventually, Timmy realized that the drums had a special mission – to spread joy, unity, and friendship through the gift of music. He played his drums in different times and places, leaving a trail of happiness wherever he went.

One day, as Timmy played a lively tune in a cheerful village square, he decided it was time to share the magic with someone else. He met a young girl who loved music as much as he did. Timmy handed her one of the magical drums, and together, they played a joyous melody that resonated through time, spreading happiness far and wide.

And so, the magical drums continued to bring joy to the hearts of children and adults alike, allowing them to travel through time and create beautiful music that transcended the ages. Timmy and his new friend became the keepers of the enchanted drums, ensuring that the magic of music would live on forever.

KEY VOCABULARY

Use context clues to determine the meaning of each term below from the text.
Next, use a device or dictionary to determine the meaning of each term.

- **majestic**

- **duo**

- **unity**

- **rhythm**

- **joyous**

Details GRAPHIC ORGANIZER

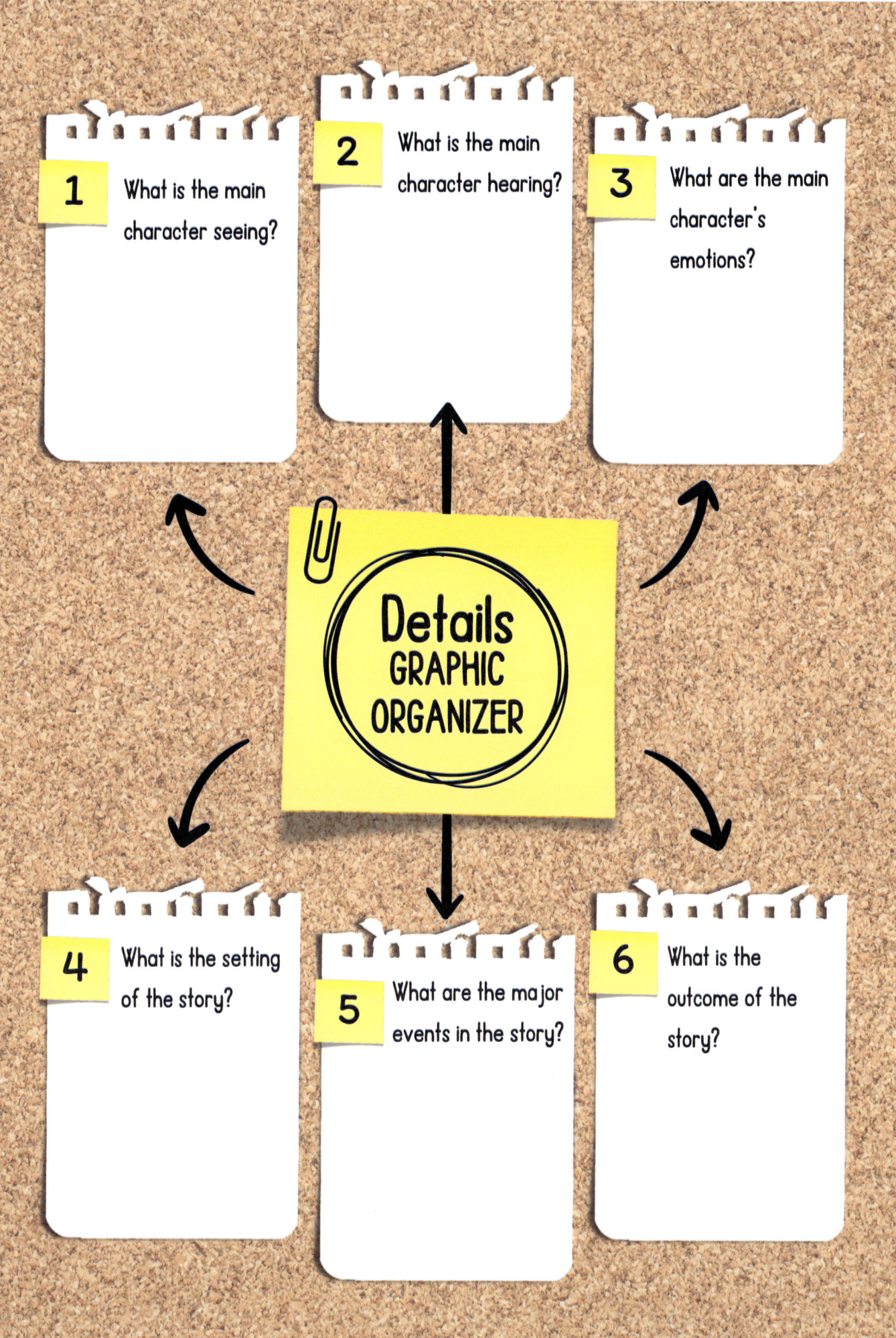

1. What is the main character seeing?

2. What is the main character hearing?

3. What are the main character's emotions?

4. What is the setting of the story?

5. What are the major events in the story?

6. What is the outcome of the story?

WRITERS' STUDIO
WEEKLY REFLECTIONS

NAME: DATE:

ACHIEVEMENTS
What were the top three things I accomplished this week?

CHALLENGES
What did I learn from facing these challenges?

GROWTH INSIGHTS
An area I want to improve is...

KEY LEARNINGS
Goals accomplished..

TIME & BALANCE
How effectively did I manage my time?

Week 5: Ella's Gift

NARRATIVE PROMPT:
Ella is about to perform in the Marbut talent show. Write a story about what happens during and after her performance.

Writers' Studio 4-Star Rubric

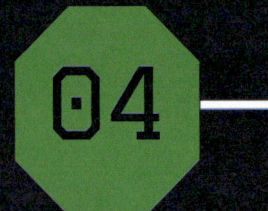

04 ★★★★

- The student's response uses the image as a stimulus to completely create a genuine or imagined experience through a well-developed narrative.
- Uses a variety of words and phrases to signal the sequence of events;
- Consistently conveys experiences or events precisely through the use of concrete words, phrases, and sensory language;
- Provides a conclusion that follows from the narrated experiences or events;
- Integrates ideas and details from source material in an effective manner;

03 ★★★

- The student's response uses the text as a trigger to create a whole narrative that describes a real or imagined experience.
- Establishes a scene and introduces one or more characters;
- lays out the events in a clear, logical sequence; employs narrative devices, like dialogue and description, to develop experiences and events or illustrate how characters react to them;
- uses words and/or phrases to denote sequence;
- conveys experiences and events with words, phrases, and details; offers a suitable resolution

02 ★★

- The student's answer, which used the image as a stimulus, is an incomplete or simplistic story.
- It attempts to use a narrative technique, such as dialogue or description, to develop experiences and events or show the responses of characters to situations.
- It introduces a vague situation and at least one character.
- It organizes events in a sequence but with some gaps or ambiguity.
- It uses sporadic signal words to indicate sequence. It uses some words or phrases inconsistently to convey experiences and events.
- Finally, it offers a weak or unclear resolution.

01 ★

- The student's response shows that they attempted to use the material as a stimulus to compose a narrative.
- The response summarises the plot; it introduces a character or scenario in a weak or basic way; it may be too short to show the whole chain of events.
- It employs language that is inappropriate, excessively simple, or unclear; it provides few, if any, words that convey experiences or events;
- it provides little to no conclusion;
- it makes little to no attempt to use dialogue or description to develop experiences and events or show the responses of characters to situations; and it may use few, if any, ideas or details from the source material.

Narrative Writer's Checklist

01	Develop a real or imagined experience.	☐
02	Include a situation and introduce a narrator and/or characters.	☐
03	Use words and phrases to show the sequence of events.	☐
04	Use dialogue and/or descriptions of actions, thoughts, and feelings to: 　o develop events. 　o show how characters respond to situations.	☐
05	Check your work for correct usage, grammar, spelling, capitalization, and punctuation.	☐
06	Organize events in order.	☐
07	Include a conclusion.	☐

NARRATIVE PROMPT:
Ella is about to perform in the Marbut talent show. Write a story about what happens during and after her performance.

Writers' Studio Storyboard
Develop a featured image for your narrative.

Title:
Medium(s) Used:

Writers' Studio Storyboard

Develop a storyboard for your narrative.

ELLA'S GIFT

Lexile Range: 810L - 1000L

Directions: Read the passage and write a summary of the main events, including details.

In the heart of Atlanta, a city known for its rich musical tapestry, lived a young jazz singer named Ella. Ella was captivated by the soulful melodies and powerful lyrics of jazz legends, particularly inspired by the great Billie Holiday. Growing up in a community that echoed with the rhythms of the civil rights movement, Ella felt a deep connection between the music she loved and the social justice issues of her time.

Ella's journey into the world of jazz began at the local community center. One day, as she was humming a jazz tune while waiting for her turn at the microphone, an elderly man named Mr. Johnson approached her. His eyes gleamed with wisdom, and he could sense the fire within Ella.

"Young lady, you've got a voice that can carry a message. Don't waste it on just any song. Sing from your heart, and let the world hear the stories that need telling," Mr. Johnson advised, handing her a worn-out record of Billie Holiday. Inspired by Mr. Johnson's words, Ella delved into the world of social justice songs, drawing inspiration from the struggles and triumphs of her community. She began singing in local clubs, weaving tales of equality, love, and resilience into her performances.

One night, as Ella was performing at a dimly lit jazz club, she caught the attention of a renowned music producer, Marcus Turner. Impressed by her soul-stirring performance, Marcus approached her after the show. "Ella, your voice has the power to move mountains. Have you ever thought about using your talent to shed light on social justice issues?" Marcus asked. Ella's eyes lit up with a newfound purpose. "That's exactly what I want to do! I want my music to mean something, to make a difference."

Under Marcus's guidance, Ella began recording an album that showcased her unique voice and her commitment to social justice. The songs spoke of racial equality, love overcoming adversity, and the hope for a better world. As the album gained traction, Ella's popularity soared, and she found herself performing on bigger stages.

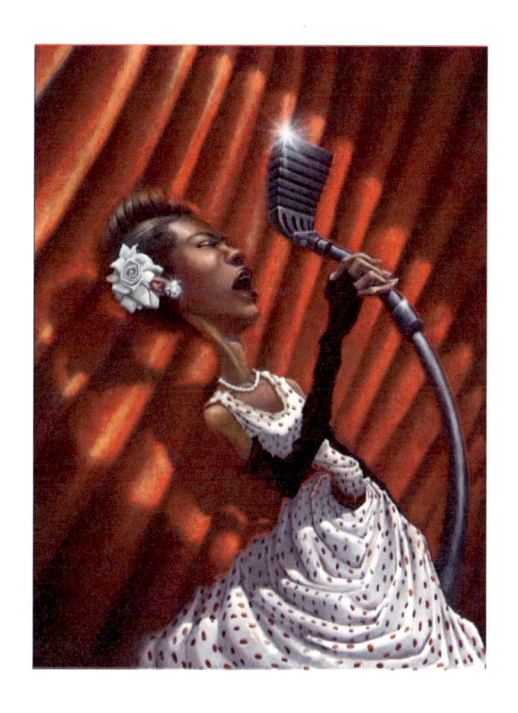

ELLA'S GIFT (CONTINUED)

Lexile Range: 1010L - 1200L

Directions: Read the passage and write a summary of the main events, including details.

One evening, Ella was backstage before a major concert, reflecting on the impact her music was having. Her phone buzzed, and a text from Mr. Johnson appeared.
"Your music is a beacon of hope, just like Billie's. Keep singing for justice, Ella. The world needs your voice."

With those words echoing in her heart, Ella stepped onto the stage. The audience fell silent as she began to sing, pouring her soul into each note. The melodies resonated with the crowd, and her lyrics sparked conversations about the pressing issues of the day. After the concert, a group of young activists approached Ella. "Your music inspires us to keep fighting for justice. Can we work together to spread awareness?" they asked.
Ella smiled, realizing that her voice had become a force for change. "Absolutely. Let's use the power of music to make a difference."

And so, Ella continued her journey as a jazz singer from Atlanta, using her music to amplify the voices of those fighting for justice. Inspired by the legacy of Billie Holiday, Ella became a beacon of hope, proving that the timeless art of jazz could be a powerful instrument for social change.

COMPREHENSION QUESTIONS

DOK 1 (Recall) Questions:

1. What is the name of the city where Ella, the jazz singer, lived? Who approached Ella after her performance at the jazz club?

DOK 2 (Understanding) Questions:

1. Describe the impact of Ella's encounter with Mr. Johnson on her musical aspirations.

2. How did Marcus Turner contribute to Ella's career as a jazz singer?

DOK 3 (Strategic Thinking) Questions:

1. How did Ella's experiences in her community shape her understanding of the connection between music and social justice?

2. Reflect on the influence of Ella's upbringing in Atlanta on her journey as a jazz singer. How did her community's historical context contribute to her musical themes and activism?

KEY VOCABULARY

Use context clues to determine the meaning of each term below from the text.
Next, use a device or dictionary to determine the meaning of each term.

- **tapestry**

- **Beacon**

- **aspirations**

- **amplify**

- **justice**

Details Graphic Organizer

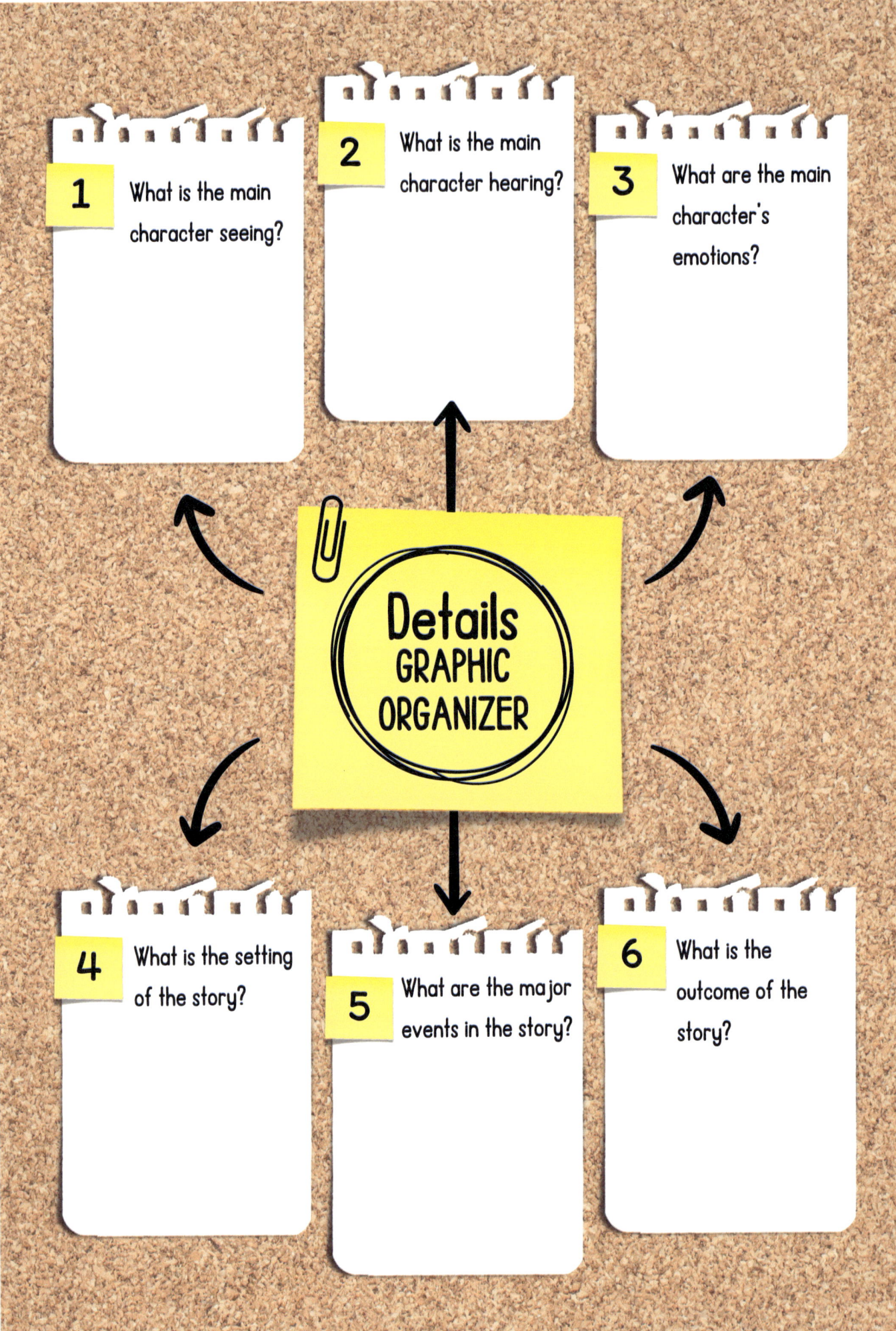

1. What is the main character seeing?

2. What is the main character hearing?

3. What are the main character's emotions?

4. What is the setting of the story?

5. What are the major events in the story?

6. What is the outcome of the story?

WRITERS' STUDIO
WEEKLY REFLECTIONS

NAME: DATE:

ACHIEVEMENTS
What were the top three things I accomplished this week?

CHALLENGES
What did I learn from facing these challenges?

GROWTH INSIGHTS
An area I want to improve is...

KEY LEARNINGS
Goals accomplished..

TIME & BALANCE
How effectively did I manage my time?

Week 6: Joe Collier and the Godfather

NARRATIVE PROMPT:
Joe has just bought a new trumpet. Write a narrative about what happens during his first week with the new instrument.

Writers' Studio 4-Star Rubric

04 ★★★★

- The student's response uses the image as a stimulus to completely create a genuine or imagined experience through a well-developed narrative.
- Uses a variety of words and phrases to signal the sequence of events;
- Consistently conveys experiences or events precisely through the use of concrete words, phrases, and sensory language;
- Provides a conclusion that follows from the narrated experiences or events;
- Integrates ideas and details from source material in an effective manner;

03 ★★★

- The student's response uses the text as a trigger to create a whole narrative that describes a real or imagined experience.
- Establishes a scene and introduces one or more characters;
- lays out the events in a clear, logical sequence; employs narrative devices, like dialogue and description, to develop experiences and events or illustrate how characters react to them;
- uses words and/or phrases to denote sequence;
- conveys experiences and events with words, phrases, and details; offers a suitable resolution

02 ★★

- The student's answer, which used the image as a stimulus, is an incomplete or simplistic story.
- It attempts to use a narrative technique, such as dialogue or description, to develop experiences and events or show the responses of characters to situations.
- It introduces a vague situation and at least one character.
- It organizes events in a sequence but with some gaps or ambiguity.
- It uses sporadic signal words to indicate sequence. It uses some words or phrases inconsistently to convey experiences and events.
- Finally, it offers a weak or unclear resolution.

01 ★

- The student's response shows that they attempted to use the material as a stimulus to compose a narrative.
- The response summarises the plot; it introduces a character or scenario in a weak or basic way; it may be too short to show the whole chain of events.
- It employs language that is inappropriate, excessively simple, or unclear; it provides few, if any, words that convey experiences or events;
- it provides little to no conclusion;
- it makes little to no attempt to use dialogue or description to develop experiences and events or show the responses of characters to situations; and it may use few, if any, ideas or details from the source material.

Narrative Writer's Checklist

01	Develop a real or imagined experience.	☐
02	Include a situation and introduce a narrator and/or characters.	☐
03	Use words and phrases to show the sequence of events.	☐
04	Use dialogue and/or descriptions of actions, thoughts, and feelings to: 　o develop events. 　o show how characters respond to situations.	☐
05	Check your work for correct usage, grammar, spelling, capitalization, and punctuation.	☐
06	Organize events in order.	☐
07	Include a conclusion.	☐

NARRATIVE PROMPT:
Joe has just bought a new trumpet. Write a narrative about what happens during his first week with the new instrument.

70

Writers' Studio Storyboard

Develop a featured image for your narrative.

Title:

Medium(s) Used:

Writers' Studio Storyboard

Develop a storyboard for your narrative.

JOE COLLIER AND THE GODFATHER

Lexile Range: 1210L-1400L
Directions: Read the passage and write a summary of the main events, including details.

The soulful city of Augusta, Georgia is a place where the echoes of jazz linger in the air. There lived a talented man named Joe Collier, a trumpeter whose notes became a bridge between the rich heritage of jazz and the pulsating rhythms of the world. Joe's journey unfolded against the backdrop of a city steeped in musical history, and little did he know that his love for the trumpet would lead him to the global stage alongside the legendary James Brown.

Joe's musical journey began at Paine College, where he honed his skills and learned the nuances of jazz that would define his signature sound. Augusta, a city with a deep connection to the roots of soul and rhythm, served as the perfect training ground for a young musician with aspirations as high as the notes he played.

Upon graduating from Paine College, Joe set his sights on a dream that would take him far beyond the borders of Augusta. The vibrant, soulful tunes that emanated from his trumpet caught the attention of none other than James Brown, the godfather of hip hop. A phone call and a momentous audition later, Joe found himself on a musical journey that would take him to stages across the globe.

As Joe joined James Brown's band, the Godfather of Soul recognized the unique talent that Joe brought to the ensemble. The first time Joe played alongside James Brown, the exchange of musical energy was palpable. The staccato bursts of the trumpet harmonized with the soulful cadence of James Brown's voice, creating a synergy that would become legendary.
"Joe, you got that fire in your trumpet that matches the fire in my soul. Let's take these tunes to places they've never been," James Brown declared with a grin, his eyes reflecting the mutual respect that would define their musical partnership.

Joe, still pinching himself to believe that he was sharing the stage with an icon, replied with gratitude, "Mr. Brown, it's an honor to play alongside you. I'm ready to take this music to the ends of the earth."

And take it they did. From the stages of Harlem to the arenas of Tokyo, Joe Collier's trumpet became a herald of the soulful revolution that was James Brown's music. The dynamic performances, the foot-stomping beats, and the electrifying energy of their collaboration became a cultural phenomenon that transcended borders and genres.

As they traveled the world, Joe absorbed not only the applause of diverse audiences but also the myriad influences of each city they visited. The streets of New Orleans, the jazz clubs of Paris, and the rhythmic markets of Rio de Janeiro – each place left an indelible mark on Joe's musical soul. His trumpet, a conduit for the emotions and experiences he absorbed, became a storyteller in its own right.

JOE COLLIER AND THE GODFATHER (CONTINUED)

Lexile Range: 1210L-1400L

Directions: Read the passage and write a summary of the main events, including details.

One evening, after a particularly exhilarating performance in London, James Brown and Joe sat down for a reflective conversation in their dressing room. The room echoed with the distant cheers of the audience and the muted sounds of the city beyond. "Joe, you're not just playing notes; you're telling a story. You're carrying the legacy of jazz and soul in that trumpet of yours. It's not just about the music; it's about the message we send, the stories we tell," James Brown remarked, his eyes reflecting the weight of a lifetime dedicated to music.

"You're right, Mr. Brown. It's about more than just the music. It's about connecting with people, touching their hearts with the language of our instruments," Joe replied, his trumpet resting beside him like a faithful companion.

Their journey together continued, a rhythmic dance through continents and cultures. Yet, as the years rolled by, Joe felt a growing desire to share his love for music beyond the concert halls and arenas. Inspired by the impact of their performances, he decided to pivot his career and channel his passion into education.

Returning to Augusta, Joe became a school teacher, determined to ignite the spark of musical curiosity in the next generation. His trumpet, once the herald of James Brown's soulful revolution, now became the beacon that guided aspiring musicians through the world of jazz. In his classroom, Joe shared not only the technicalities of trumpet playing but also the stories of his global adventures with James Brown. His students, wide-eyed and eager, listened as Joe weaved tales of the jazz clubs in Harlem, the lively streets of Havana, and the enchanting melodies of the African plains.

One day, Joe received a call from Karen Gordon, a fellow musician and educator, and Benito Reeves, a percussionist with a passion for teaching. They shared Joe's vision of bringing the magic of jazz and the arts to schools around the country. Together, they formed a group dedicated to jazz education, traveling from school to school, sharing their experiences and imparting the rich legacy of jazz to eager students.

In one of their workshops at a local school, the trio engaged students in a lively dialogue about the origins of jazz. Joe's trumpet resonated through the auditorium, carrying the essence of the jazz clubs in New Orleans and the vibrant energy of their global performances.

A student raised their hand, curiosity gleaming in their eyes. "Mr. Collier, what was it like playing with James Brown? How did it feel to be part of something so big?" Joe smiled, the memories of those transcendent moments flooding back. "Playing with Mr. Brown was like riding a musical hurricane. It wasn't just about the notes; it was about the energy, the passion, and the belief that music could change the world. And you know what? It did."

JOE COLLIER AND THE GODFATHER (CONTINUED)

Lexile Range: 1210L-1400L

Directions: Read the passage and write a summary of the main events, including details.

As the workshop unfolded, Joe, Karen, and Benito encouraged the students to pick up instruments, to let the rhythms of jazz and the arts become a part of their own stories. The trio's efforts were not just about education; it was a mission to inspire the next generation, to nurture the seeds of creativity and passion that lay within each young soul.

In the quiet moments between workshops, Joe reflected on the evolution of his journey. From the streets of Augusta to the global stages with James Brown, and now in the classrooms of aspiring musicians, his trumpet had been a constant companion. Its notes, once heard in the pulsating heart of soul music, now resonated in the eager minds of children discovering the beauty of jazz.

As the trio traveled from city to city, school to school, the impact of their workshops became evident. Students who had never touched an instrument found a rhythm within themselves. The spirit of jazz, with its improvisation and creative freedom, became a source of empowerment for the young minds touched by Joe, Karen, and Benito.

In the twilight of his career, Joe Collier found fulfillment not only in the echoes of his trumpet but in the spark of inspiration ignited in the eyes of the students he encountered. His journey, from the global stages with James Brown to the classrooms of eager learners, had come full circle.

As the trio concluded one of their workshops in a small town, a student approached Joe with a heartfelt question, "Mr. Collier, do you think I could ever play like you?"

Joe chuckled warmly, his trumpet by his side. "You can play better than me, young one. Your journey is just beginning, and who knows where your trumpet will take you."

In that moment, as the notes of the trumpet lingered in the air, Joe Collier, the soulful trumpeter from Augusta, felt the resonance of a lifelong melody that transcended time and place. His legacy wasn't just in the music he played but in the hearts he inspired and the stories he shared – a living testament to the transformative power of jazz, the arts, and the enduring spirit of a trumpet that had journeyed from the streets of Augusta to the world and back again.

COMPREHENSION QUESTIONS

DOK 1 (Recall) Questions:

1. Where did Joe Collier start his musical journey?

2. What instrument did Joe play?

3. Who is considered the godfather of hip hop, and with whom did Joe Collier perform?

4. Where did Joe Collier graduate from?

5. What role did Karen Gordon and Benito Reeves play in Joe Collier's educational endeavors?

DOK 2 (Understanding) Questions:

1. Explain the significance of Augusta, Georgia, in shaping Joe Collier's musical development.

2. How did Joe Collier describe the synergy between his trumpet and James Brown's voice?

3. What inspired Joe Collier to transition from a performer to an educator?

4. How did Joe Collier integrate his global experiences with James Brown into his teaching methods?

5. Why did Joe Collier, Karen Gordon, and Benito Reeves decide to form a group dedicated to jazz education?

COMPREHENSION QUESTIONS

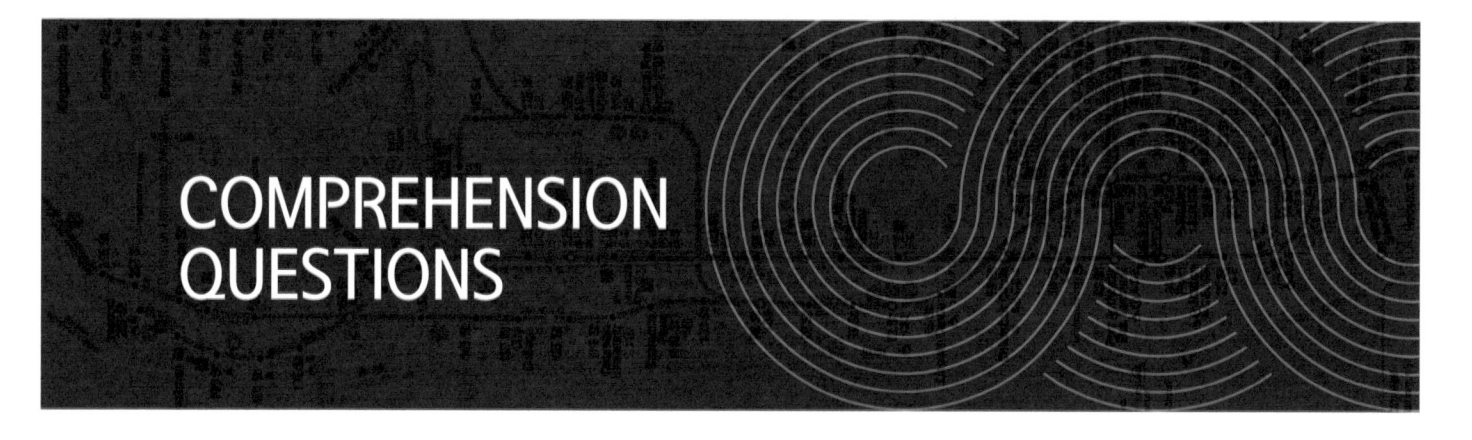

DOK 3 (Strategic Thinking) Questions:

1. Analyze the impact of Joe Collier's trumpet on the global stage with James Brown. How did this experience shape his perspective on music and education?

2. Reflect on Joe Collier's decision to become a school teacher. How did he leverage his experiences to inspire the next generation of musicians?

3. Evaluate the effectiveness of the trio's approach to jazz education in schools. How did their workshops impact students, and what broader implications does this have for arts education?

DOK 4 (Extended Thinking) Questions:

1. Imagine you are a student in one of Joe Collier's workshops. How might his experiences with James Brown influence your own approach to music and creativity?

2. Consider the challenges Joe Collier might have faced transitioning from the global stage to local classrooms. How did he overcome these challenges, and what can other educators learn from his journey?

3. If you were to continue Joe Collier's legacy, how would you incorporate jazz and the arts into education to inspire future generations?

KEY VOCABULARY

Use context clues to determine the meaning of each term below from the text.
Next, use a device or dictionary to determine the meaning of each term.

- **indelible**

- **synergy**

- **cadence**

- **conduit**

- **palpable**

Details GRAPHIC ORGANIZER

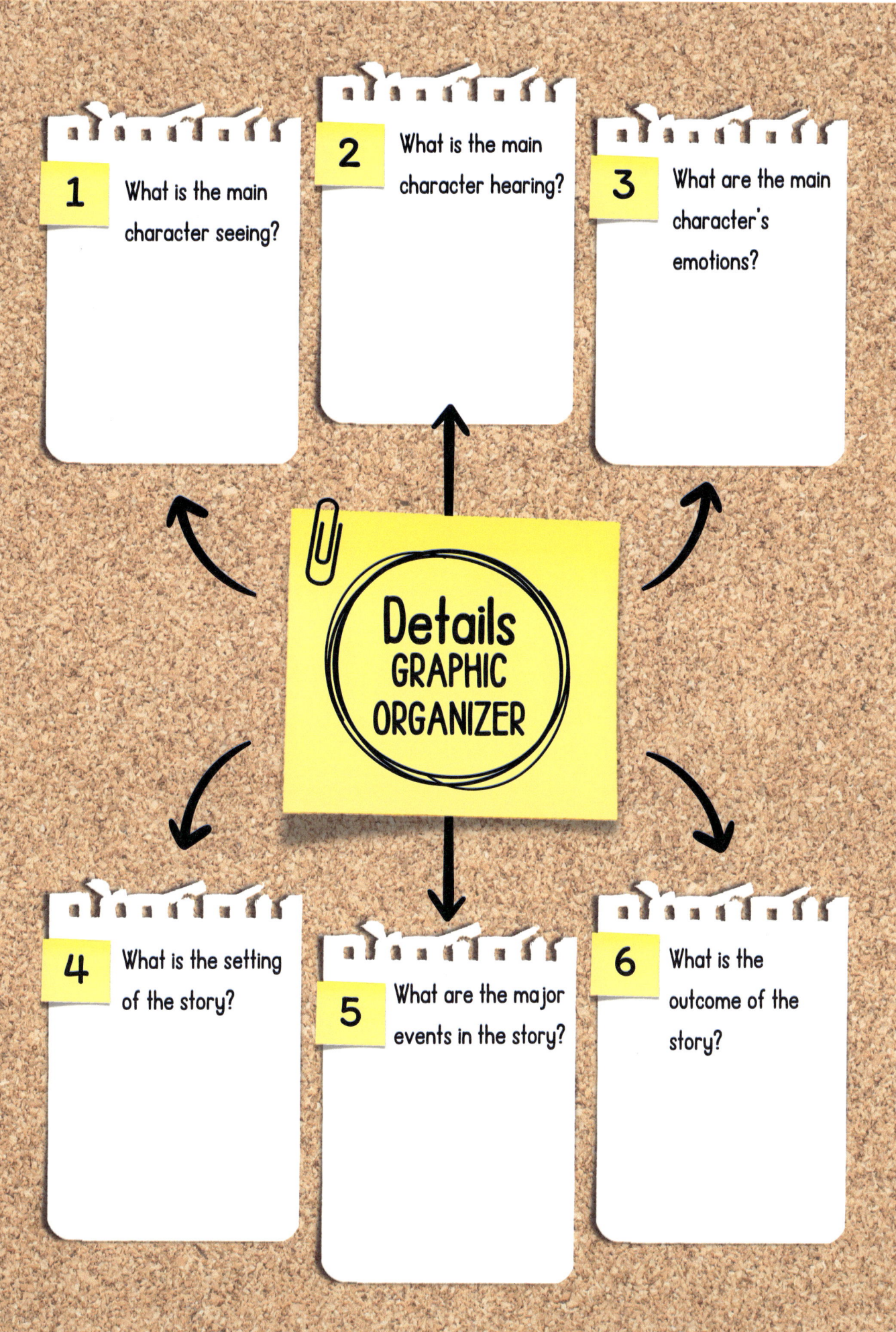

1. What is the main character seeing?

2. What is the main character hearing?

3. What are the main character's emotions?

4. What is the setting of the story?

5. What are the major events in the story?

6. What is the outcome of the story?

WRITERS' STUDIO
WEEKLY REFLECTIONS

NAME: DATE:

ACHIEVEMENTS
What were the top three things I accomplished this week?

CHALLENGES
What did I learn from facing these challenges?

GROWTH INSIGHTS
An area I want to improve is...

KEY LEARNINGS
Goals accomplished..

TIME & BALANCE
How effectively did I manage my time?

Week 7: Carlos and the Collection

NARRATIVE PROMPT:
Write a story about a DJ who is preparing to enter a music competition. Write a story about what he does to prepare and the outcome of the competition.

Writers' Studio 4-Star Rubric

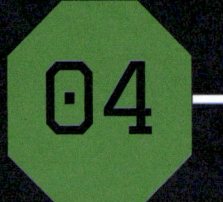

04 ★★★★

- The student's response uses the image as a stimulus to completely create a genuine or imagined experience through a well-developed narrative.
- Uses a variety of words and phrases to signal the sequence of events;
- Consistently conveys experiences or events precisely through the use of concrete words, phrases, and sensory language;
- Provides a conclusion that follows from the narrated experiences or events;
- Integrates ideas and details from source material in an effective manner;

03 ★★★

- The student's response uses the text as a trigger to create a whole narrative that describes a real or imagined experience.
- Establishes a scene and introduces one or more characters;
- lays out the events in a clear, logical sequence; employs narrative devices, like dialogue and description, to develop experiences and events or illustrate how characters react to them;
- uses words and/or phrases to denote sequence;
- conveys experiences and events with words, phrases, and details; offers a suitable resolution

02 ★★

- The student's answer, which used the image as a stimulus, is an incomplete or simplistic story.
- It attempts to use a narrative technique, such as dialogue or description, to develop experiences and events or show the responses of characters to situations.
- It introduces a vague situation and at least one character.
- It organizes events in a sequence but with some gaps or ambiguity.
- It uses sporadic signal words to indicate sequence. It uses some words or phrases inconsistently to convey experiences and events.
- Finally, it offers a weak or unclear resolution.

01 ★

- The student's response shows that they attempted to use the material as a stimulus to compose a narrative.
- The response summarises the plot; it introduces a character or scenario in a weak or basic way; it may be too short to show the whole chain of events.
- It employs language that is inappropriate, excessively simple, or unclear; it provides few, if any, words that convey experiences or events;
- it provides little to no conclusion;
- it makes little to no attempt to use dialogue or description to develop experiences and events or show the responses of characters to situations; and it may use few, if any, ideas or details from the source material.

Narrative Writer's Checklist

- Develop a real or imagined experience. ☐

- Include a situation and introduce a narrator and/or characters. ☐

- Use words and phrases to show the sequence of events. ☐

- Use dialogue and/or descriptions of actions, thoughts, and feelings to: ☐
    - o develop events.
    - o show how characters respond to situations.

- Check your work for correct usage, grammar, spelling, capitalization, and punctuation. ☐

- Organize events in order. ☐

- Include a conclusion. ☐

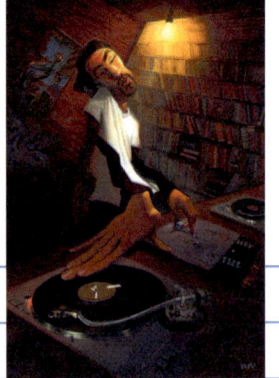

NARRATIVE PROMPT:

Write a story about a DJ who is preparing to enter a music competition. Write a story about what he does to prepare and the outcome of the competition.

Writers' Studio Storyboard

Develop a featured image for your narrative.

Title:

Medium(s) Used:

Writers' Studio Storyboard

Develop a storyboard for your narrative.

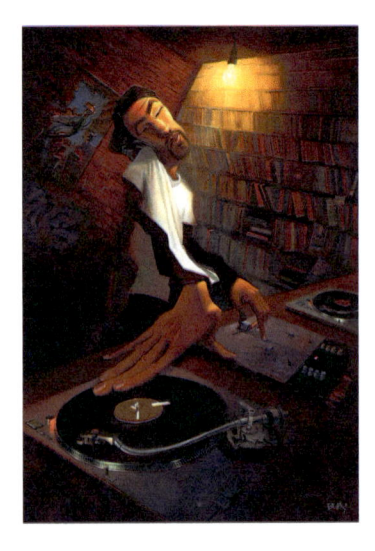

CARLOS AND THE COLLECTION

Lexile Range: 1010L - 1200L

Directions: Read the passage and write a summary of the main events, including details.

The neighborhood of Harlem is a place where the rhythm of the streets intertwines with the soulful beats of the city. Carlos was a Puerto Rican DJ with an unwavering passion for music. Growing up in the vibrant cultural tapestry of Harlem, Carlos found solace and inspiration in the syncopated melodies of hip hop and the timeless harmonies of jazz remixes.

From a young age, Carlos was drawn to the turntables and the art of mixing, allowing him to create sonic landscapes that reflected the eclectic spirit of his surroundings. His diverse heritage infused his mixes with a unique fusion of Puerto Rican rhythms and the raw energy of Harlem's streets. This sonic journey became his personal canvas, where he painted the stories of his community through beats and breaks.

However, Carlos wasn't just a DJ; he was a passionate student at a local performing arts school. Here, he honed his craft, delving into the intricacies of music theory and production. His days were a harmonious blend of academic pursuit and creative expression, a testament to his dedication to mastering the art of sound.

Harlem's streets, though rich in culture, were not without challenges. Peer pressure lurked in the corners, tempting Carlos to conform to societal expectations. However, Carlos found his refuge in the pulsating heart of music. The turntables became not only his instruments but also his armor against the pressures of his environment.

While his peers succumbed to the allure of conformity, Carlos remained steadfast in his pursuit of musical excellence. His passion for hip hop and jazz remixes became a source of strength, a channel through which he resisted the pull of negative influences. The beats that echoed through the streets were a testament to his resilience, a declaration that he would chart his own course, driven by the music that flowed through his veins.

Carlos' story is a melody of resistance, a testament to the transformative power of passion. In the midst of societal pressures, he found his voice in the rhythms that defined him. As he continued to spin records and create harmonies that echoed through Harlem's streets, Carlos became not just a DJ but a living embodiment of the cultural mosaic that is Harlem.

COMPREHENSION QUESTIONS

DOK 2 (Understanding) Questions:

1. How does the passage describe Carlos's connection to music and the role it plays in his life?

2. Explain how Carlos's diverse heritage influences the music he creates as a DJ. What elements does he incorporate into his mixes?

DOK 3 (Strategic Thinking) Questions:

1. Analyze the significance of Carlos being a passionate student at a performing arts school. How does his academic pursuit contribute to his creative expression, and why is this important in the context of the story?

2. Consider the role of peer pressure in Harlem's streets and Carlos's response to it. How does his passion for hip hop and jazz remixes serve as a form of resistance, and what does this reveal about his character and values?

KEY VOCABULARY

Use context clues to determine the meaning of each term below from the text.
Next, use a device or dictionary to determine the meaning of each term.

- **syncopated**

- **eclectic**

- **resilience**

- **intricacies**

- **embodiment**

Details Graphic Organizer

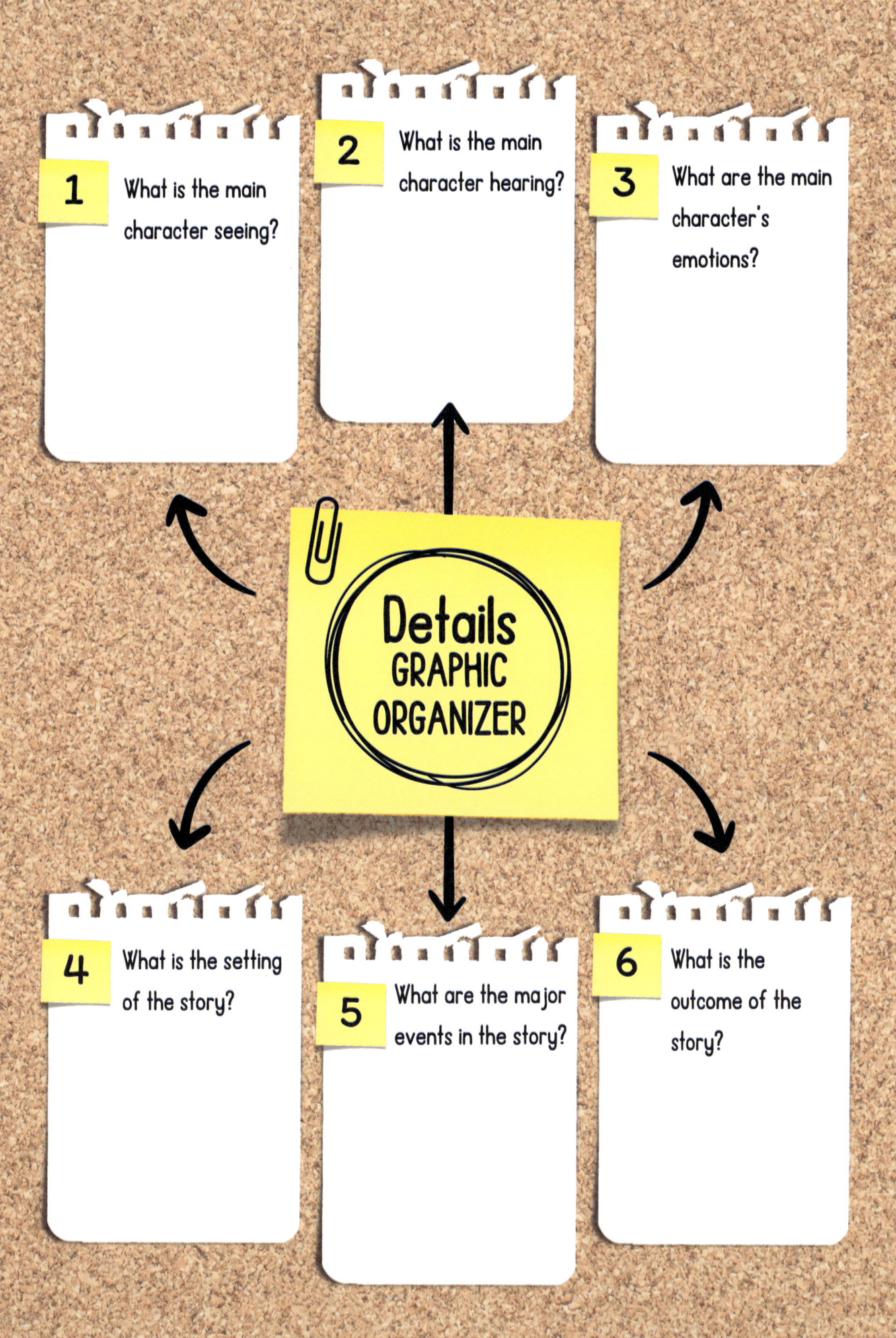

1. What is the main character seeing?

2. What is the main character hearing?

3. What are the main character's emotions?

4. What is the setting of the story?

5. What are the major events in the story?

6. What is the outcome of the story?

WRITERS' STUDIO
WEEKLY REFLECTIONS

NAME: DATE:

ACHIEVEMENTS
What were the top three things I accomplished this week?

CHALLENGES
What did I learn from facing these challenges?

GROWTH INSIGHTS
An area I want to improve is...

KEY LEARNINGS
Goals accomplished..

TIME & BALANCE
How effectively did I manage my time?

Week #8: Jazz, Hip-Hop and the Brownstone's Timeless Echo

NARRATIVE PROMPT:

A family has just arrived at their new home in Harlem. Write a story about their first day in their new building.

Writers' Studio 4-Star Rubric

04 ★★★★
- The student's response uses the image as a stimulus to completely create a genuine or imagined experience through a well-developed narrative.
- Uses a variety of words and phrases to signal the sequence of events;
- Consistently conveys experiences or events precisely through the use of concrete words, phrases, and sensory language;
- Provides a conclusion that follows from the narrated experiences or events;
- Integrates ideas and details from source material in an effective manner;

03 ★★★
- The student's response uses the text as a trigger to create a whole narrative that describes a real or imagined experience.
- Establishes a scene and introduces one or more characters;
- lays out the events in a clear, logical sequence; employs narrative devices, like dialogue and description, to develop experiences and events or illustrate how characters react to them;
- uses words and/or phrases to denote sequence;
- conveys experiences and events with words, phrases, and details; offers a suitable resolution

02 ★★
- The student's answer, which used the image as a stimulus, is an incomplete or simplistic story.
- It attempts to use a narrative technique, such as dialogue or description, to develop experiences and events or show the responses of characters to situations.
- It introduces a vague situation and at least one character.
- It organizes events in a sequence but with some gaps or ambiguity.
- It uses sporadic signal words to indicate sequence. It uses some words or phrases inconsistently to convey experiences and events.
- Finally, it offers a weak or unclear resolution.

01 ★
- The student's response shows that they attempted to use the material as a stimulus to compose a narrative.
- The response summarises the plot; it introduces a character or scenario in a weak or basic way; it may be too short to show the whole chain of events.
- It employs language that is inappropriate, excessively simple, or unclear; it provides few, if any, words that convey experiences or events;
- it provides little to no conclusion;
- it makes little to no attempt to use dialogue or description to develop experiences and events or show the responses of characters to situations; and it may use few, if any, ideas or details from the source material.

Narrative Writer's Checklist

01	Develop a real or imagined experience.	☐
02	Include a situation and introduce a narrator and/or characters.	☐
03	Use words and phrases to show the sequence of events.	☐
04	Use dialogue and/or descriptions of actions, thoughts, and feelings to: 　o develop events. 　o show how characters respond to situations.	☐
05	Check your work for correct usage, grammar, spelling, capitalization, and punctuation.	☐
06	Organize events in order.	☐
07	Include a conclusion.	☐

NARRATIVE PROMPT:
A family has just arrived at their new home in Harlem. Write a story about their first day in their new building.

Writers' Studio Storyboard

Develop a featured image for your narrative.

Title:
Medium(s) Used:

Writers' Studio Storyboard

Develop a storyboard for your narrative.

JAZZ, HIP-HOP AND THE BROWNSTONE'S TIMELESS ECHO

Lexile Range: 1010L - 1200L

Directions: Read the passage and write a summary of the main events, including details.

Harlem is a neighborhood known for its rich culture, grounded in music and art. At the end of a long ride through Manhattan stood the brownstone at 17 East 126th Street. Unassuming in its facade, this residence would etch its name in history as the backdrop of one of the most iconic photographs in the jazz world—a timeless snapshot of the luminaries who shaped the soundscape of an era. Captured by Art Kane in 1958, this photograph not only immortalized the faces of jazz legends but also embodied the spirit of an art form that would later pave the way for the rhythmic genius of hip hop.

On that fateful day in 1958, the stoop of the brownstone became a stage where jazz orchestras and individual musicians gathered, breaking free from the constraints of sheet music and traditional arrangements. The air buzzed with the improvisational energy that defined the jazz movement—a movement that was not just a genre but a cultural revolution.

As Art Kane orchestrated the composition of this historic photograph, the brownstone served as a canvas where the notes and personalities of jazz collided. Musicians of unparalleled skill and creativity lined the steps, creating a living tableau of the jazz renaissance. The photograph was more than a collection of faces; it was a testament to the diversity of styles and personalities that coexisted in the jazz milieu.

The significance of this photograph extends beyond the mere assembly of musicians. A closer look reveals the presence of children, playing carefree amidst the gathering of artistic genius. Their laughter and spontaneous movements capture the essence of the moment—a moment when jazz was not confined to concert halls but spilled into the streets, creating an organic tapestry of sound and life.

This image, frozen in time, represents the vibrant crossroads of a musical evolution. Just as the brownstone at 17 East 126th Street housed the improvisational symphony of jazz, the streets of Harlem echoed with the organic beats of a culture finding its voice. Jazz, with its commitment to improvisation and originality, became a forerunner to the genius that would later define the rhythms and wordplay of hip hop. Jazz, like hip hop, thrived on the brilliance of its creators—the visionaries who transformed everyday narratives into musical masterpieces. The brownstone at the center of this photograph was a microcosm of this creative explosion, a gathering place for minds that challenged conventions and birthed a revolution in sound.

The legacy of jazz transcended its era, becoming a wellspring of inspiration for future generations. Modern hip hop artists, including the likes of Rakim and Pete Rock, found themselves drawn to the jazz catalogs of yesteryear. The improvisational spirit, the emphasis on individuality, and the intricate layering of sounds—all hallmarks of jazz—became a source of creative nourishment for the burgeoning hip hop movement.
As the photograph captured the indelible faces of jazz luminaries like Dizzy Gillespie, Thelonious Monk, and Count Basie, it also documented the convergence of cultures and genres. The brownstone, witness to this convergence, stood as a living testament to the idea that artistic brilliance knows no boundaries.

JAZZ, HIP-HOP AND THE BROWNSTONE'S TIMELESS ECHO

Lexile Range: 1010L - 1200L

Directions: Read the passage and write a summary of the main events, including details.

The streets of Harlem, where the sounds of jazz wafted through the air, bore witness to a cultural renaissance that echoed in the beats of hip hop decades later. The brownstone at 17 East 126th Street, with its weathered stoop and unassuming exterior, became a symbol of the transformative power of art. It was not merely a residence; it was a crucible where the alchemy of creativity unfolded, birthing a musical legacy that reverberates through time.

In the realm of hip hop, where artists craft verses like poets and beats like maestros, the influence of jazz is undeniable. The improvisational prowess of a saxophone mirrored in the lyrical dexterity of an emcee; the rhythmic complexity of a drum solo resonating in the sampled beats of a DJ—jazz and hip hop share a spiritual kinship that transcends the boundaries of time.

As hip hop evolved, jazz remained a guiding light, offering a blueprint for artistic innovation. The brownstone, its stoop an altar for jazz's congregational celebration, became a beacon for those who sought to push the boundaries of musical expression. The children playing in the photograph, oblivious to the weight of the moment, embodied the continuity of creativity—a passing of the torch from one generation to the next. The brownstone at 17 East 126th Street was more than a physical location; it was a crucible where artistic innovation bubbled to the surface. The collaboration, camaraderie, and sheer genius that permeated the gathering of jazz legends on that stoop echoed in the narratives of hip hop pioneers who, decades later, would find inspiration in the improvisational spirit of their predecessors.

In the annals of musical history, the brownstone stands as a hallowed ground—a place where the echoes of jazz blended seamlessly with the emerging beats of hip hop. It serves as a reminder that creativity is not confined by time or genre; rather, it is a continuum, an ever-evolving symphony that builds upon the foundations laid by those who came before.

The photograph taken that day in 1958 freezes a moment in time—a moment when the brownstone, the musicians, and the children became conduits for the spirit of jazz. And just as the brownstone witnessed the birth of a musical revolution, its echoes reverberate in the pulsating heart of hip-hop, where the genius of improvisation and originality continues to shape lives in Harlem and beyond.

COMPREHENSION QUESTIONS

DOK 1 (Recall) Questions:

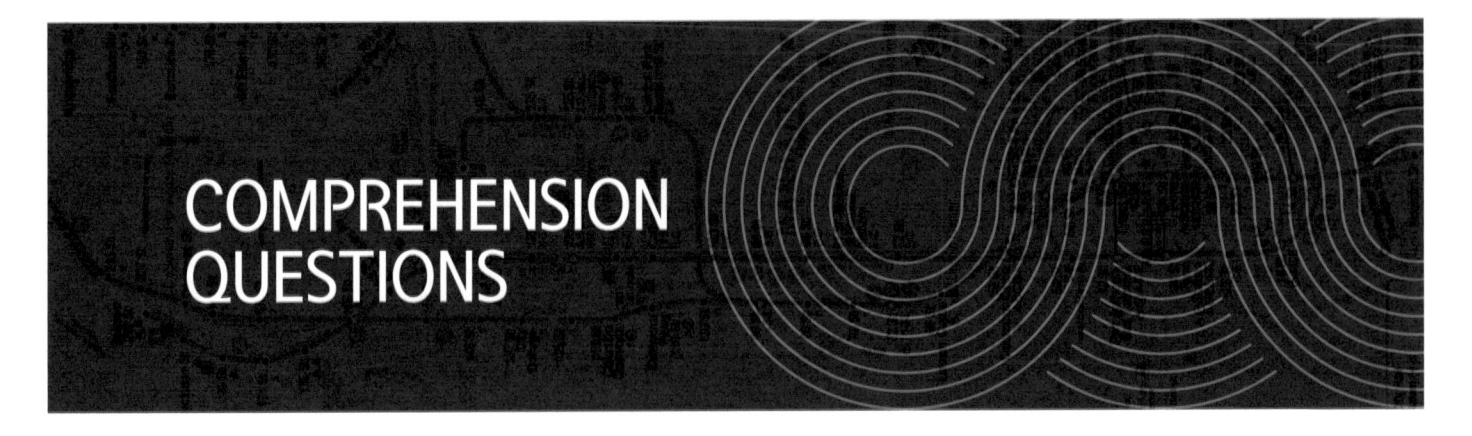

1. Who captured the iconic photograph at 17 East 126th Street in 1958?

2. What was the significance of the brownstone's stoop in the photograph?

3. Name two jazz luminaries featured in the historic 1958 photograph.

4. What artistic movement is often credited as a forerunner to hip hop?

5. In what ways did jazz and hip hop share a spiritual kinship?

DOK 2 (Understanding) Questions:

1. Explain the cultural and improvisational significance of the brownstone in Harlem during the jazz era.

2. How did the photograph at 17 East 126th Street capture the essence of jazz's diversity and creativity?

3. Describe the role of the children in the photograph and their symbolic representation.

4. In what aspects did jazz influence modern hip hop, as mentioned in the passage?

5. How did the brownstone become a microcosm of creative explosion during the jazz renaissance?

COMPREHENSION QUESTIONS

DOK 3 (Strategic Thinking) Questions:

1. Analyze the parallels between the gathering at the brownstone in 1958 and the emerging beats of hip hop. How did one influence the other?

2. Evaluate the impact of the photograph in shaping the narrative of jazz history and its continued influence on hip-hop.

3. Consider the cultural convergence depicted in the photograph. How did it reflect the broader context of artistic and societal changes in the 1950s?

4. Reflect on the role of improvisation in both jazz and hip hop. How did this shared aspect contribute to the evolution of music?

DOK 4 (Extended Thinking) Questions:

1. Imagine you are a musician present at the brownstone in 1958. How might you describe the atmosphere and collaboration during that historic gathering?

2. Explore the potential impact of the brownstone's cultural legacy on future artistic movements beyond hip-hop. How could it inspire new forms of creativity?

3. If you were curating an exhibition about the intersection of jazz and hip hop, how would you incorporate the brownstone photograph into the narrative?

4. Consider the societal implications of jazz's influence on hip hop. How has this cultural exchange shaped perceptions of music and creativity?

KEY VOCABULARY

Use context clues to determine the meaning of each term below from the text.
Next, use a device or dictionary to determine the meaning of each term.

- **luminaries**

- **orchestrated**

- **renaissance**

- **symphony**

- **microcosm**

Details Graphic Organizer

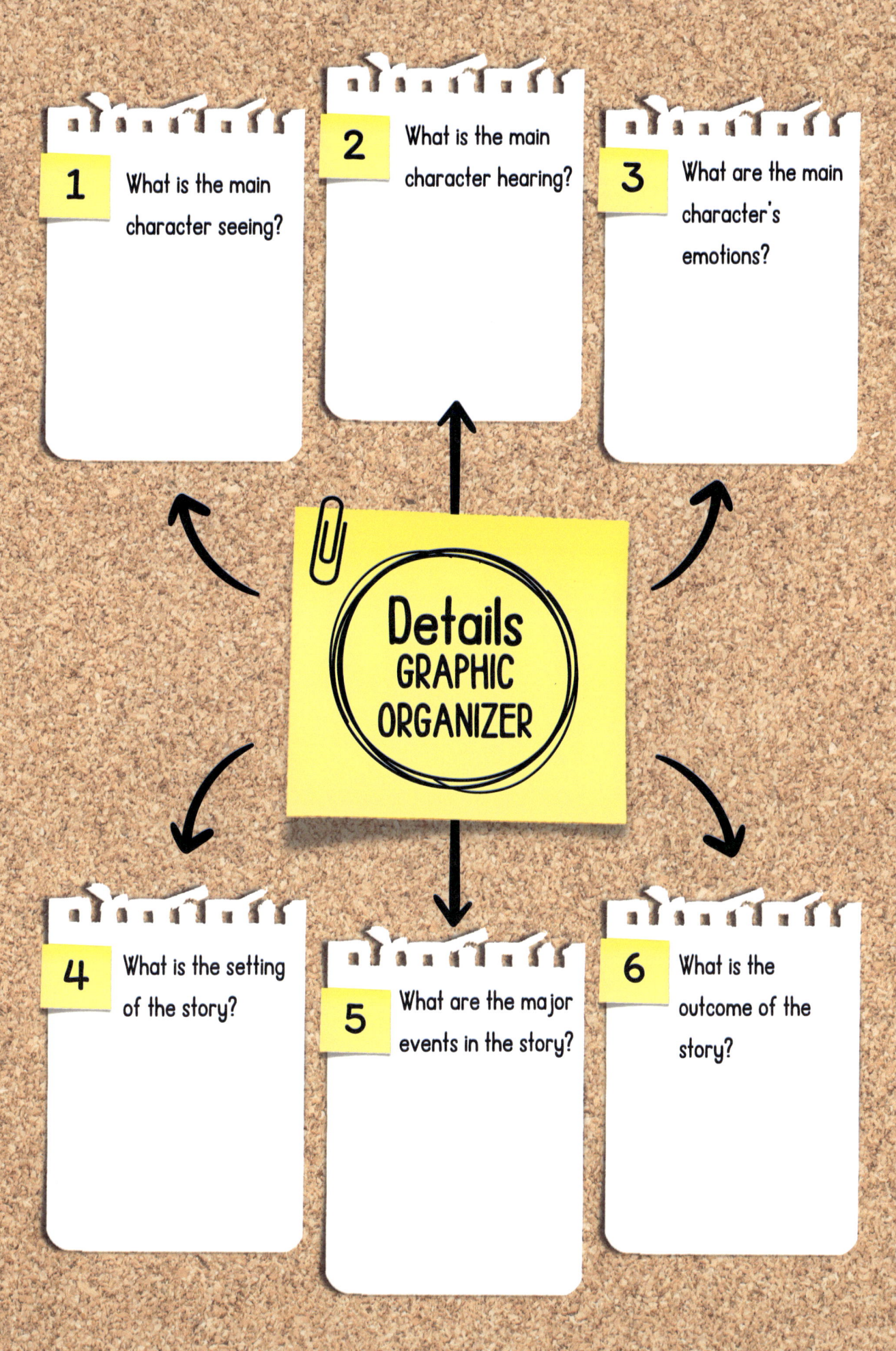

1. What is the main character seeing?

2. What is the main character hearing?

3. What are the main character's emotions?

4. What is the setting of the story?

5. What are the major events in the story?

6. What is the outcome of the story?

Week 9: Jeffrey's Journey

NARRATIVE PROMPT:

Write a story about an artist who enters a trainyard with a bag filled with spray paint. Tell what happens over the next several hours.

Writers' Studio 4-Star Rubric

04 ★★★★

- The student's response uses the image as a stimulus to completely create a genuine or imagined experience through a well-developed narrative.
- Uses a variety of words and phrases to signal the sequence of events;
- Consistently conveys experiences or events precisely through the use of concrete words, phrases, and sensory language;
- Provides a conclusion that follows from the narrated experiences or events;
- Integrates ideas and details from source material in an effective manner;

03 ★★★

- The student's response uses the text as a trigger to create a whole narrative that describes a real or imagined experience.
- Establishes a scene and introduces one or more characters;
- lays out the events in a clear, logical sequence; employs narrative devices, like dialogue and description, to develop experiences and events or illustrate how characters react to them;
- uses words and/or phrases to denote sequence;
- conveys experiences and events with words, phrases, and details; offers a suitable resolution

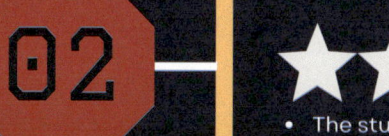

02 ★★

- The student's answer, which used the image as a stimulus, is an incomplete or simplistic story.
- It attempts to use a narrative technique, such as dialogue or description, to develop experiences and events or show the responses of characters to situations.
- It introduces a vague situation and at least one character.
- It organizes events in a sequence but with some gaps or ambiguity.
- It uses sporadic signal words to indicate sequence. It uses some words or phrases inconsistently to convey experiences and events.
- Finally, it offers a weak or unclear resolution.

01 ★

- The student's response shows that they attempted to use the material as a stimulus to compose a narrative.
- The response summarises the plot; it introduces a character or scenario in a weak or basic way; it may be too short to show the whole chain of events.
- It employs language that is inappropriate, excessively simple, or unclear; it provides few, if any, words that convey experiences or events;
- it provides little to no conclusion;
- it makes little to no attempt to use dialogue or description to develop experiences and events or show the responses of characters to situations; and it may use few, if any, ideas or details from the source material.

Narrative Writer's Checklist

| 01 | Develop a real or imagined experience. | ☐ |

| 02 | Include a situation and introduce a narrator and/or characters. | ☐ |

| 03 | Use words and phrases to show the sequence of events. | ☐ |

| 04 | Use dialogue and/or descriptions of actions, thoughts, and feelings to:
　　o develop events.
　　o show how characters respond to situations. | ☐ |

| 05 | Check your work for correct usage, grammar, spelling, capitalization, and punctuation. | ☐ |

| 06 | Organize events in order. | ☐ |

| 07 | Include a conclusion. | ☐ |

NARRATIVE PROMPT:
Write a story about an artist who enters a trainyard with a bag filled with spray paint. Tell what happens over the next several hours.

Writers' Studio Storyboard

Develop a featured image for your narrative.

Title:
Medium(s) Used:

Writers' Studio Storyboard

Develop a storyboard for your narrative.

JEFFREY'S JOURNEY

Lexile Range: 1010L - 1200L

Directions: Read the passage and write a summary of the main events, including details.

What extraordinary fusion of talents resided within Jeffrey, the graffiti virtuoso in the electric core of Harlem, where every street corner hums with the rhythm of the city? His narrative is a symphony of creative flair, mathematical finesse, and an unbreakable tie to the soul of hip hop culture, all set against the vibrant tapestry of the bustling cityscape.

Jeffrey's story began with the rhythmic beats of hip hop echoing through the streets, creating a canvas upon which he would eventually paint his life. Raised in a neighborhood where creativity and resilience danced in harmony, Jeffrey discovered his passion for graffiti at an early age. The walls of Harlem became his gallery, and spray paint his chosen medium.

Yet, amidst the kaleidoscope of colors and intricate designs, Jeffrey harbored an unexpected love – mathematics. It wasn't just numbers and equations for him; it was a language that resonated in the precision of lines and angles. As he adorned walls with vibrant graffiti, he found geometric patterns weaving through his art, creating a visual symphony that echoed the mathematical principles he admired.

Harlem, a nurturing cocoon for artistic endeavors, also provided the cultural backdrop that fueled Jeffrey's creativity. The culture of hip hop, with its raw storytelling and rebellious spirit, became the muse for his graffiti. Each stroke of the spray can, each vibrant hue, told a story of resilience and creativity deeply rooted in the rhythm of Harlem's streets.

As Jeffrey's artistic prowess flourished, so did his academic pursuits. Recognizing the harmony between his love for graffiti and mathematics, he delved into both worlds with equal fervor. He pursued a dual degree in Fine Arts and Mathematics, a seemingly unconventional combination that would later define the unique trajectory of his career.

Jeffrey's journey took an unexpected turn when he received an acceptance letter from Morehouse College in Atlanta, a prestigious institution known for its commitment to academic excellence and the rich tapestry of African American culture. Leaving Harlem behind, he found himself in the embrace of the Southern charm and academic rigor of Morehouse.

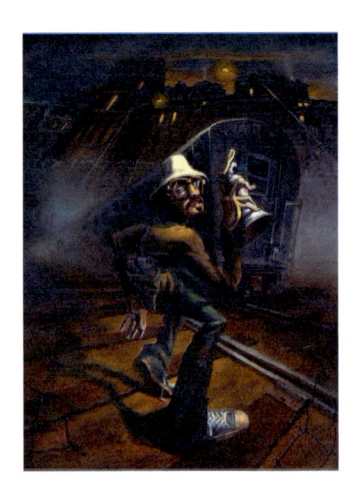

JEFFREY'S JOURNEY (CONTINUED)

Lexile Range: 1010L - 1200L

Directions: Read the passage and write a summary of the main events, including details.

As a student at Morehouse, Jeffrey's dual passions continued to thrive. He found mentors who appreciated the interdisciplinary nature of his pursuits, encouraging him to explore the intersections between art and mathematics. Morehouse became the crucible where Jeffrey forged his identity as an artist, a mathematician, and a proud advocate for hip hop culture.

Upon graduating with honors, Jeffrey faced a crossroads – a decision that would shape his future. Armed with a degree in Fine Arts and Mathematics, he chose a path less traveled. Rather than pursuing a conventional career in either field, Jeffrey decided to create his own narrative, one that seamlessly blended the worlds of art, mathematics, and hip hop.

Returning to Atlanta, Jeffrey settled in Lithonia, a vibrant suburb that provided the perfect backdrop for his eclectic interests. He immersed himself in the local arts scene, contributing not only with his graffiti but also with his newfound role as an educator. Jeffrey became a beacon for aspiring artists, demonstrating that the pursuit of passion need not conform to traditional boundaries.

In Lithonia, Jeffrey established the Hip Hop Literacy Lab, a haven for young minds eager to explore their artistic and mathematical potentials. The lab wasn't just a classroom; it was a playground where graffiti met geometry, and beats harmonized with equations. Through innovative workshops, Jeffrey inspired students to see the beauty in the connections between seemingly disparate disciplines.

Word of Jeffrey's transformative approach spread beyond Lithonia. His work at the intersection of art, mathematics, and hip hop garnered attention, and Morehouse College took notice. Recognizing the profound impact he could have on students, the college invited Jeffrey to join its faculty.ding light for those who dared to defy the boundaries of conventional wisdom. In the quiet rhythm of the Southern night, the echoes of Jeffrey's journey reverberated – a melody of resilience, creativity, and the transformative power of pursuing one's true passions.

JEFFREY'S JOURNEY (CONTINUED)

Lexile Range: 1010L - 1200L

Directions: Read the passage and write a summary of the main events, including details.

As a professor at Morehouse, Jeffrey brought a fresh perspective to the academic landscape. His classes became a dynamic exploration of the symbiotic relationship between art and mathematics. Graffiti, once considered a form of rebellion, became a legitimate medium for mathematical expression. Jeffrey's enthusiasm was contagious, and his students, much like the graffiti that adorned the walls of Harlem, embraced the unexpected beauty in the marriage of art and mathematics.

But Jeffrey's impact extended beyond the classroom. He continued to paint murals that adorned the Atlanta skyline, each stroke a testament to the rich cultural heritage that informed his art. His graffiti became a bridge between the historic roots of hip-hop and the academic corridors of Morehouse. The Hip Hop Literacy Lab flourished under Jeffrey's guidance, nurturing a generation of artists who saw the world through the lens of geometric precision and lyrical storytelling. The lab became a testament to the transformative power of unconventional education, where graffiti, hip-hop, and mathematics converged to inspire and empower.

In the heart of Atlanta, Jeffrey's story unfolded as a living testament to the harmony that could exist between seemingly disparate disciplines. His journey, from the graffiti-covered walls of Harlem to the academic halls of Morehouse College, encapsulated the essence of creativity unbound by convention.

As the sun set over Lithonia, casting a warm glow on the murals that adorned the city, Jeffrey stood proud, knowing that his passion for graffiti, mathematics, and hip-hop had not only shaped his life but had become a guiding light for those who dared to defy the boundaries of conventional wisdom. In the quiet rhythm of the Southern night, the echoes of Jeffrey's journey reverberated – a melody of resilience, creativity, and the transformative power of pursuing one's true passions.

COMPREHENSION QUESTIONS

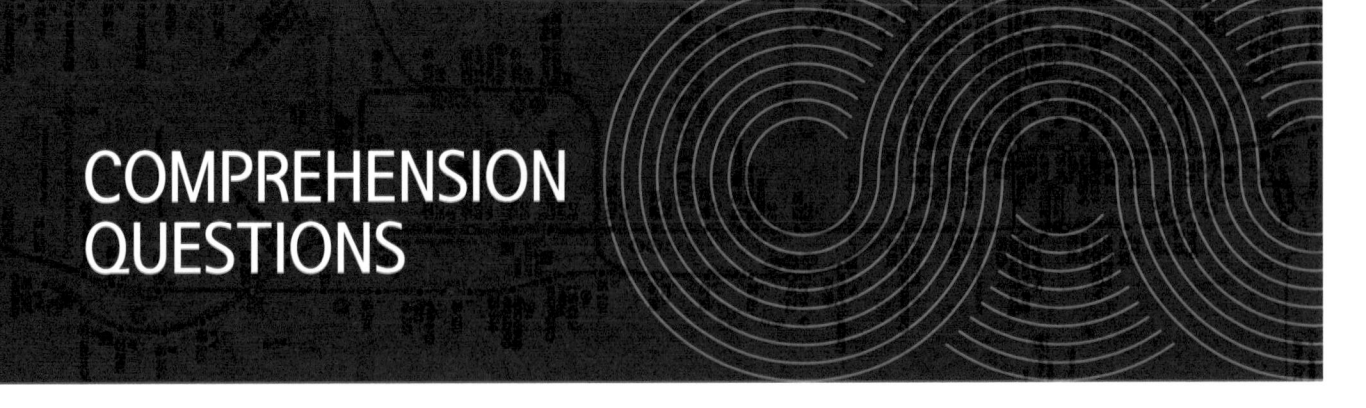

DOK 2 (Understanding) Questions:

1. Explain the role of Harlem in shaping Jeffrey's early artistic endeavors and how his graffiti evolved as a reflection of the hip hop culture in the neighborhood.

2. Describe the dual passions that drove Jeffrey's academic pursuits at Morehouse College. How did he perceive the connection between mathematics and graffiti art?

DOK 3 (Strategic Thinking) Questions:

1. Analyze the decision-making process that led Jeffrey to create the Hip Hop Literacy Lab in Lithonia. How did this initiative reflect his commitment to merging art, mathematics, and hip hop culture?

2. Reflect on Jeffrey's impact as an educator at Morehouse College. In what ways did he integrate his unique perspective on the convergence of art and mathematics into his teaching methods, and how did this influence his students?

DOK 4 (Extended Thinking) Questions:

1. Evaluate the significance of Jeffrey's decision to blend the worlds of art, mathematics, and hip hop in his career. How did this interdisciplinary approach contribute to his personal and professional growth, and what broader implications does it have for education and creativity?

2. Imagine the potential challenges Jeffrey faced in establishing the Hip Hop Literacy Lab and integrating unconventional teaching methods. How did he overcome these challenges, and what can other educators learn from his innovative approach to teaching?

KEY VOCABULARY

Use context clues to determine the meaning of each term below from the text.
Next, use a device or dictionary to determine the meaning of each term.

- **insatiable**

- **cocoon**

- **prowess**

- **trajectory**

- **rigor**

Details Graphic Organizer

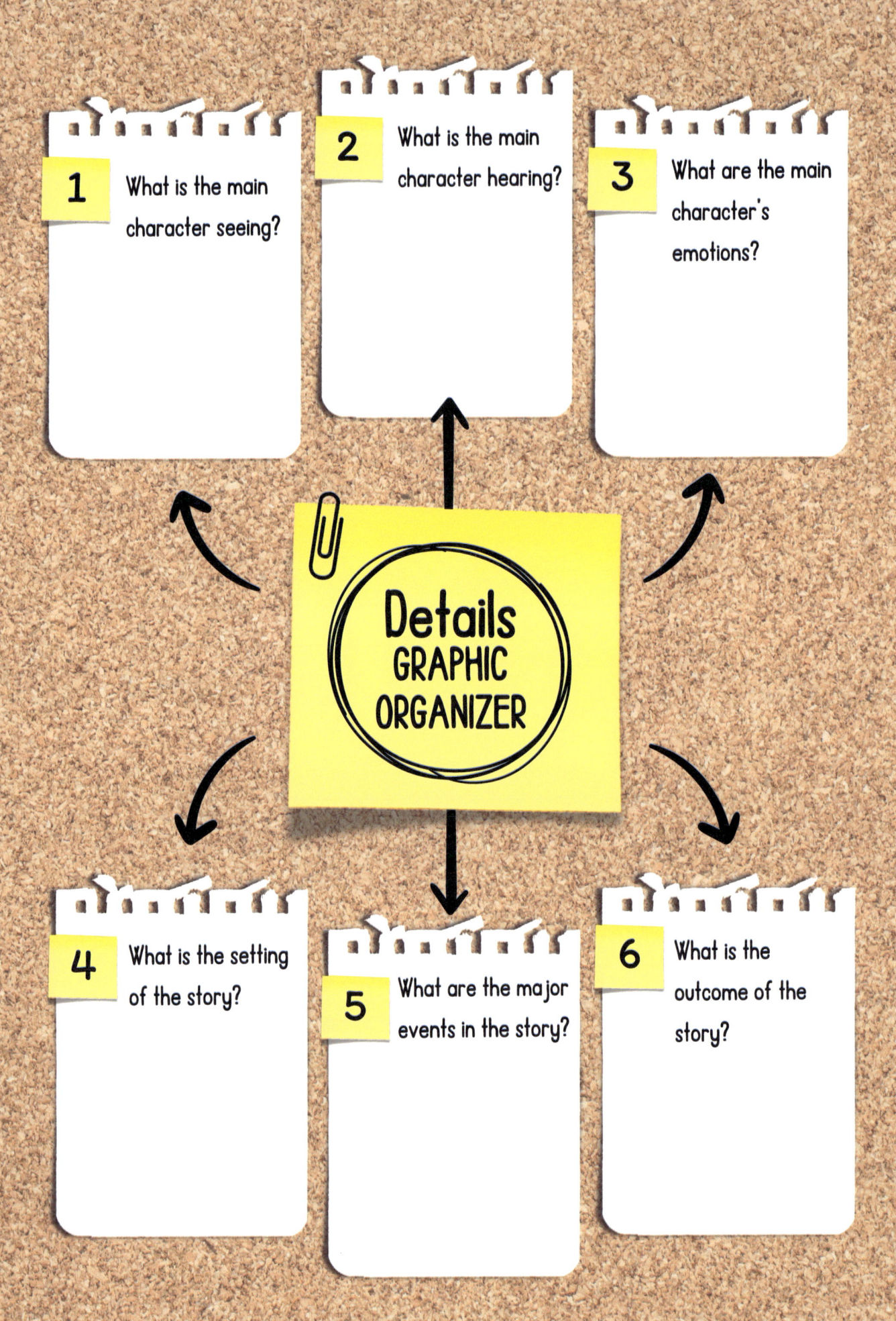

1. What is the main character seeing?

2. What is the main character hearing?

3. What are the main character's emotions?

4. What is the setting of the story?

5. What are the major events in the story?

6. What is the outcome of the story?

WRITERS' STUDIO
WEEKLY REFLECTIONS

NAME: DATE:

ACHIEVEMENTS
What were the top three things I accomplished this week?

CHALLENGES
What did I learn from facing these challenges?

GROWTH INSIGHTS
An area I want to improve is...

KEY LEARNINGS
Goals accomplished..

TIME & BALANCE
How effectively did I manage my time?

Week 10: Coastal Dreams

Writers' Studio 4-Star Rubric

04 ★★★★

- The student's response uses the image as a stimulus to completely create a genuine or imagined experience through a well-developed narrative.
- Uses a variety of words and phrases to signal the sequence of events;
- Consistently conveys experiences or events precisely through the use of concrete words, phrases, and sensory language;
- Provides a conclusion that follows from the narrated experiences or events;
- Integrates ideas and details from source material in an effective manner;

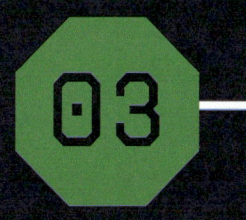

03 ★★★

- The student's response uses the text as a trigger to create a whole narrative that describes a real or imagined experience.
- Establishes a scene and introduces one or more characters;
- lays out the events in a clear, logical sequence; employs narrative devices, like dialogue and description, to develop experiences and events or illustrate how characters react to them;
- uses words and/or phrases to denote sequence;
- conveys experiences and events with words, phrases, and details; offers a suitable resolution

02 ★★

- The student's answer, which used the image as a stimulus, is an incomplete or simplistic story.
- It attempts to use a narrative technique, such as dialogue or description, to develop experiences and events or show the responses of characters to situations.
- It introduces a vague situation and at least one character.
- It organizes events in a sequence but with some gaps or ambiguity.
- It uses sporadic signal words to indicate sequence. It uses some words or phrases inconsistently to convey experiences and events.
- Finally, it offers a weak or unclear resolution.

01 ★

- The student's response shows that they attempted to use the material as a stimulus to compose a narrative.
- The response summarises the plot; it introduces a character or scenario in a weak or basic way; it may be too short to show the whole chain of events.
- It employs language that is inappropriate, excessively simple, or unclear; it provides few, if any, words that convey experiences or events;
- it provides little to no conclusion;
- it makes little to no attempt to use dialogue or description to develop experiences and events or show the responses of characters to situations; and it may use few, if any, ideas or details from the source material.

Narrative Writer's Checklist

01	Develop a real or imagined experience.	☐
02	Include a situation and introduce a narrator and/or characters.	☐
03	Use words and phrases to show the sequence of events.	☐
04	Use dialogue and/or descriptions of actions, thoughts, and feelings to: 　o develop events. 　o show how characters respond to situations.	☐
05	Check your work for correct usage, grammar, spelling, capitalization, and punctuation.	☐
06	Organize events in order.	☐
07	Include a conclusion.	☐

NARRATIVE PROMPT:

Hannah Lauren is a talented singer, rapper, and actress. She wants to decide if she should focus on just one of her passions or pursue them all. Write a story about what happens next.

Writers' Studio Storyboard

Develop a featured image for your narrative.

Title:
Medium(s) Used:

Writers' Studio Storyboard

Develop a storyboard for your narrative.

COASTAL DREAMS

Lexile Range: 1010L - 1200L

Directions: Read the passage and write a summary of the main events, including details.

In the serene coastal town of St. Simons, Georgia, nestled under the shade of ancient oaks and serenaded by the whispers of the ocean breeze, lived a young woman named Hannah Lauren. With sun-kissed skin and eyes that held the secrets of the sea, Hannah possessed a gift that stirred souls and painted melodies in the air – she was a talented guitar singer.

From the age of six, Hannah's fingers danced effortlessly along the strings of her beloved guitar, weaving tales of love, loss, and the beauty of the world around her. Her voice, like honey dripping from a golden spoon, carried a warmth that enveloped listeners and transported them to distant shores.

But beneath the tranquility of St. Simons lay a fire that burned bright within Hannah. Inspired by the raw energy of the bustling cityscape, she yearned to explore new horizons and carve her name into the fabric of a world beyond her coastal haven. Her father, a dedicated teacher in Atlanta, had always been her biggest supporter, encouraging her to pursue her dreams with unwavering belief. With her guitar slung over her shoulder and her father's words echoing in her heart, Hannah set her sights on Brooklyn, New York – the pulsating heart of creativity and diversity.

As she stepped onto the crowded streets of her new neighborhood, she felt the beat of the city resonate through her bones, igniting a passion that she had never known before. In the vibrant tapestry of Brooklyn, Hannah's musical journey took an unexpected turn.

Immersed in the rich culture of hip hop, she found herself drawn to the rhythmic cadence of the streets and the raw honesty of its storytellers. With each strum of her guitar and every lyric that flowed from her lips, Hannah discovered a new voice – one that blended the soulful melodies of her roots with the vibrant energy of hip hop.

COASTAL DREAMS (CONTINUED)

Lexile Range: 1010L - 1200L

Directions: Read the passage and write a summary of the main events, including details.

Her performances became legendary in the streets of Brooklyn, drawing crowds from far and wide who were captivated by the magic that she wove with her music. From dimly lit cafes to bustling street corners, Hannah's acoustic interpretations of hip hop classics became anthems for a new generation, earning her the title of an icon in her newfound home.

But amidst the adoration and acclaim, Hannah remained true to herself – a girl from St. Simons with a guitar in her hands and a heart full of dreams. And as she strummed beneath the glow of Brooklyn's neon lights, she knew that her journey was just beginning – a symphony of notes waiting to be played, a story waiting to be told.

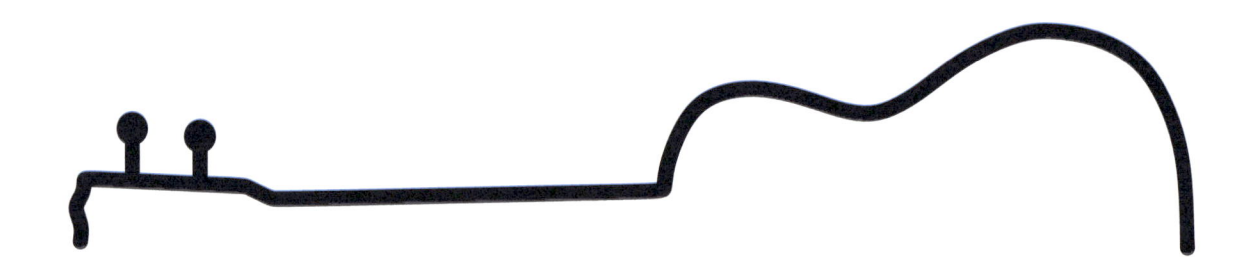

COMPREHENSION QUESTIONS

DOK 2 (Understanding) Questions:

1. How does Hannah's upbringing in St. Simons influence her musical journey in Brooklyn?

2. What role does Hannah's father play in shaping her aspirations and supporting her pursuit of her dreams?

DOK 3 (Strategic Thinking) Question:

1. Analyze the significance of Hannah's fusion of acoustic guitar music with hip hop culture. How does this blend of genres contribute to her success as an artist in Brooklyn?

2. Evaluate the theme of cultural identity and adaptation in Hannah's story. How does she navigate the transition from her coastal hometown to the vibrant streets of Brooklyn, and how does this impact her artistic expression and sense of self?

Details Graphic Organizer

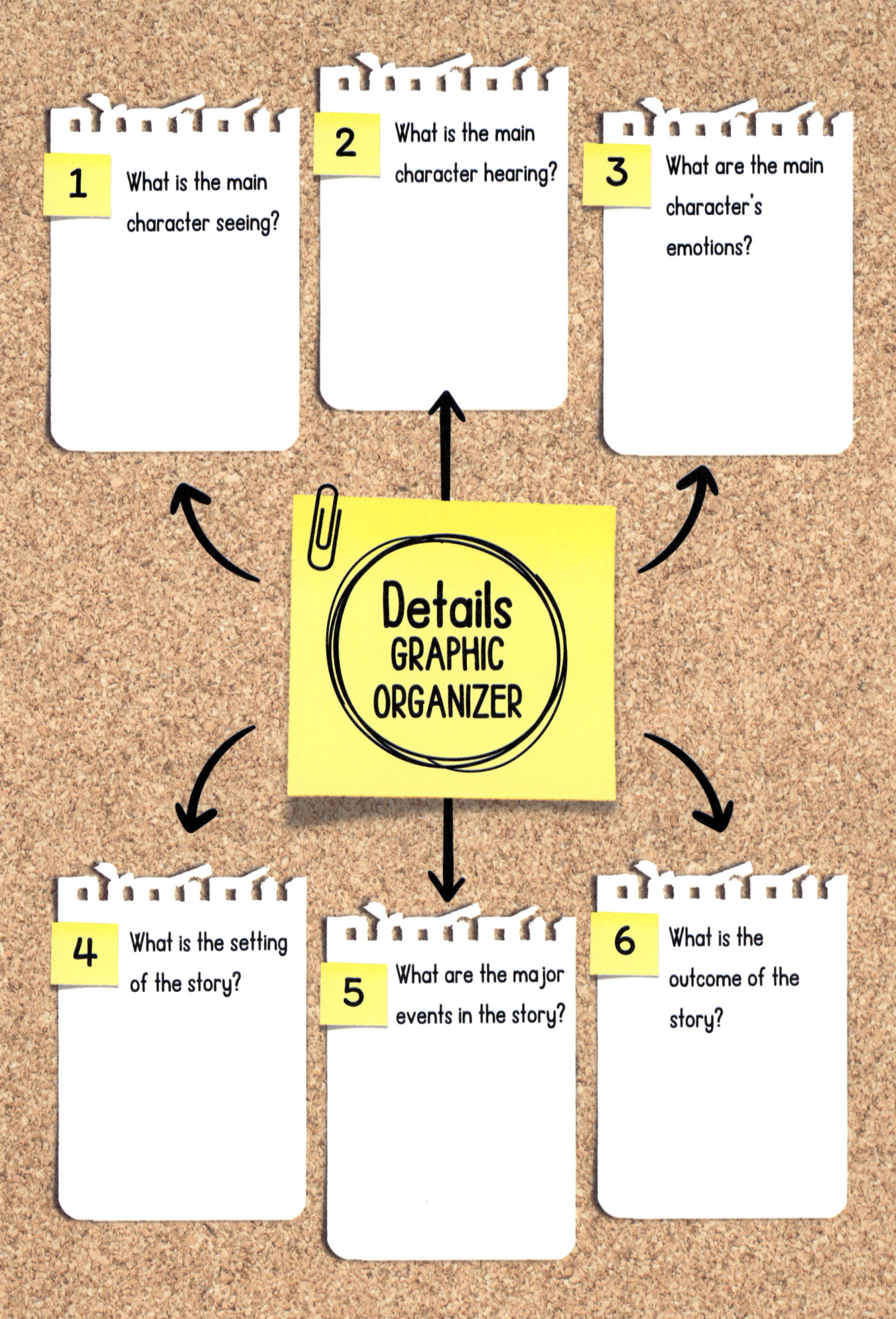

1. What is the main character seeing?

2. What is the main character hearing?

3. What are the main character's emotions?

4. What is the setting of the story?

5. What are the major events in the story?

6. What is the outcome of the story?

WRITERS' STUDIO
WEEKLY REFLECTIONS

NAME: DATE:

ACHIEVEMENTS
What were the top three things I accomplished this week?

CHALLENGES
What did I learn from facing these challenges?

GROWTH INSIGHTS
An area I want to improve is...

KEY LEARNINGS
Goals accomplished..

TIME & BALANCE
How effectively did I manage my time?

Writers' Studio

Embark on a transformative journey into the world of storytelling with "Writers' Studio," an innovative workbook designed for elementary and middle school writing students. This groundbreaking resource, a collaboration of renowned artist Justin Bua and acclaimed educator André Benito Mountain, introduces a dynamic fusion of arts integration and hip hop pedagogy to revolutionize narrative writing.

"The Writers' Studio" seamlessly blends the visual power of images by Justin Bua with meticulously researched activities that elevate students' writing and comprehension skills. This workbook isn't just a guide; it's a creative space where young writers can explore and refine their narrative talents.

Inside "The Writers' Studio," students will find engaging exercises that inspire vivid storytelling. The workbook goes beyond conventional approaches by incorporating areas for students to create visuals and storyboards, allowing them to bring their narratives to life visually.

André Benito Mountain, a trailblazer in bringing hip-hop pedagogy to schools for literacy support, introduces a landmark achievement in arts integration and culturally responsive teaching. "The Writers' Studio" is not just a workbook; it's a significant step forward, marrying the worlds of literature, visual arts, and hip-hop in a harmonious dance of creativity and education. Join the movement, unlock your imagination, and enhance your narrative writing skills with "The Writers' Studio." It's more than a book; it's a revolution in the way we teach, learn, and express ourselves.

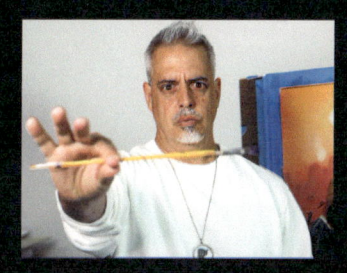

Born in 1968 in NYC's untamed Upper West Side and raised between Manhattan and East Flatbush, Brooklyn, groundbreaking artist Justin Bua was fascinated by the raw, visceral street life of the city. He attended the Fiorello H. LaGuardia High School of Music and Performing Arts and complemented his education on the streets by writing graffiti and performing worldwide with breakdancing crews. Bua went on to the Art Center College of Design in Pasadena, California where he earned a B.F.A in Illustration.

André Benito Mountain is an elementary principal in the metro Atlanta area and founder of Def-Education Consulting LLC. Andre is the host of the Def-Education Podcast on Spotify, the publisher of Def-Ed Magazine, and the creator of the Hip Hop Literacy Laboratory. He has written for EdWeek, Education Post, Citizen Ed, Urban Pro Weekly, and Teach Magazine. He has collaborated with hip hop legend Masta Ace to create lessons for teachers to integrate socially conscious hip hop into their lessons for elementary and middle school students. He and his family reside in Atlanta, Georgia.

DEF-ED & BUA

Made in the USA
Columbia, SC
02 June 2024